Carlisle Citadel Sta

150 years a Railway C
Denis Perriam & David Ra

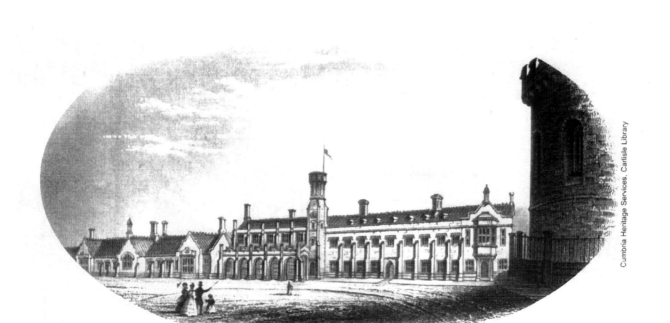

P3 Publications

British Library Cataloguing in Publication Data
A catalogue record for this book is available from the British Library.
ISBN 0 9522098 - 7 - X

First published in Great Britain in 1998 by:-

P3 Publications

13 Beaver Road
Carlisle
Cumbria
CA2 7PS

The original print run sold out at the beginning of 2013.

Due to requests for further copies this was followed by a limited print run of 200 copies in 2013, produced by scanning the original book and printing in monochrome only. The original book was part colour, part monochrome.

This second limited print run was produced in 2016.

Front Cover Illustration:
A reconstructional drawing by the late John Robinson of the Citadel Station as it would have appeared in 1880. The inset is a coloured postcard circa 1904.

Opposite:
An engraving of Citadel Station in 1847

Carlisle Citadel Station

150 years a Railway Centre
Denis Perriam & David Ramshaw

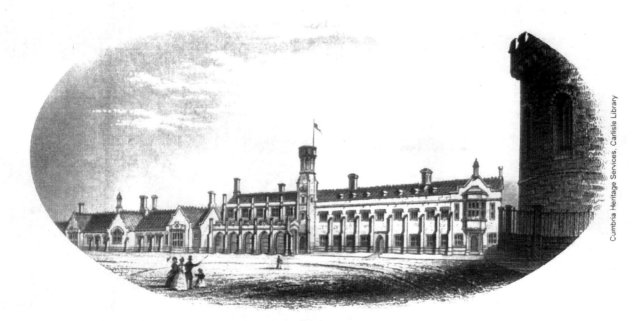

Cumbria Heritage Services, Carlisle Library

Introduction and Acknowledgments

In 1996 Denis Perriam was commissioned by Tullie House Museum to develop ideas for an exhibition to commemorate the 150 year anniversary of the Citadel Station in 1997. When the exhibition was staged in the museum, constraints of space and expense prevented many of the submitted themes being followed through.

As the research had already been done, it was felt by the authors that a more permanent record of the history of the station should be produced. This opportunity has been taken to present in book form, most of the material used in the exhibition and also what was ultimately left out. We gratefully acknowledge the full co-operation of the staff at Tullie House in the project and permission to reproduce items from the collection there. Thanks are also due to those who loaned exhibits and where these are reproduced they are individually acknowledged. Special thanks must go to the staffs of Cumbria Heritage Services at the Record Office, Carlisle and Carlisle Library, for their patience and help with our researches.

Any books which have touched on the history of the station have been aimed at those already interested in railways. Most of these are illustrated with photographs of steam locomotives. This book has a more unconventional approach looking at social history aspects and drawing on a wealth of sources of illustrations which have not been seen before. We gratefully acknowledge permission given by the Cumbrian Newspaper Group to reproduce newspaper photographs from their publications which help to bring the station to life. Where pictures were lacking, John Robinson has expertly recreated scenes which give insight not previously available. The picture story book approach will have a wide appeal and make this publication much more accessible to those not normally interested in such a subject. Each reproduction which is not in the authors' collection is acknowledged and thanks are given to all those who have helped to make this book a success, especially Peter W Robinson, Alistair Leslie, John Huggon, Ashley Kendall, Ian Parsons and Gary Swainson.

Most railway terms and abbreviations are explained in the text, but it may be useful for those not familiar with railway terminology to know that trains went 'up' to London and 'down' to Glasgow.

June 1998

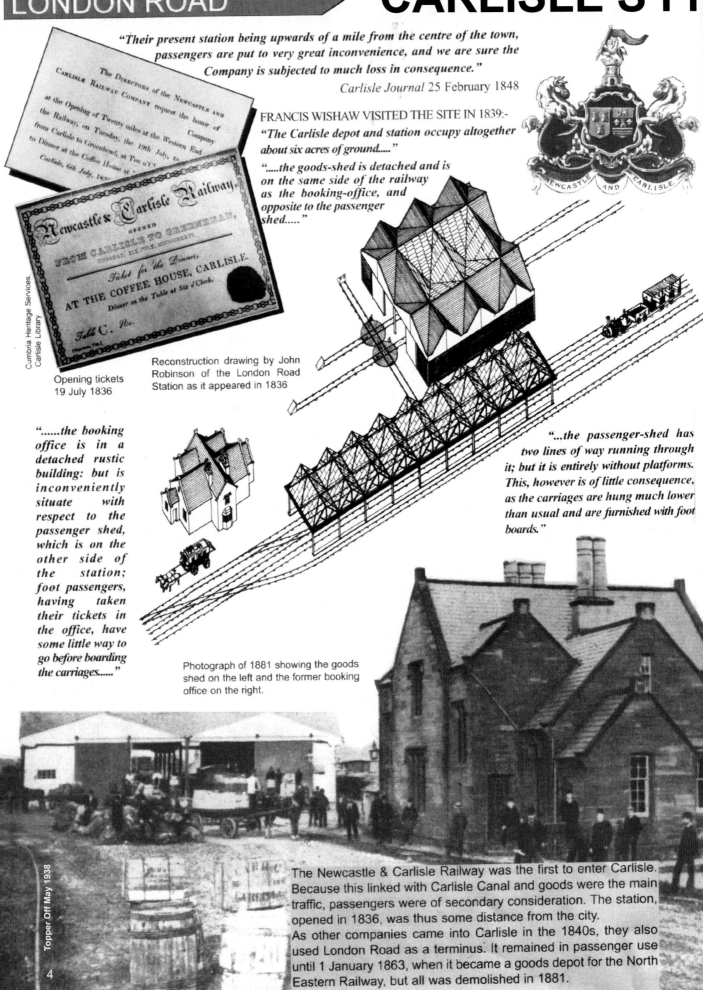

"Their present station being upwards of a mile from the centre of the town, passengers are put to very great inconvenience, and we are sure the Company is subjected to much loss in consequence."

Carlisle Journal 25 February 1848

FRANCIS WISHAW VISITED THE SITE IN 1839:-

"The Carlisle depot and station occupy altogether about six acres of ground....."

".....the goods-shed is detached and is on the same side of the railway as the booking-office, and opposite to the passenger shed....."

The Directors of the Newcastle and Carlisle Railway Company request the honor of Company at the Opening of Twenty miles at the Western End of the Railway, on Tuesday, the 19th July, to Dinner at the Coffee House at Carlisle. 6th July, 1836.

Newcastle & Carlisle Railway,

OPENED

FROM CARLISLE TO GREENHEAD,

TUESDAY, XIX JULY, MDCCCXXXVI.

Ticket for the Dinner,

AT THE COFFEE HOUSE, CARLISLE.

Dinner on the Table at Six o'Clock.

Table C. No.

Opening tickets 19 July 1836

Reconstruction drawing by John Robinson of the London Road Station as it appeared in 1836

"......the booking office is in a detached rustic building: but is inconveniently situate with respect to the passenger shed, which is on the other side of the station; foot passengers, having taken their tickets in the office, have some little way to go before boarding the carriages......"

"...the passenger-shed has two lines of way running through it; but it is entirely without platforms. This, however is of little consequence, as the carriages are hung much lower than usual and are furnished with foot boards."

Photograph of 1881 showing the goods shed on the left and the former booking office on the right.

The Newcastle & Carlisle Railway was the first to enter Carlisle. Because this linked with Carlisle Canal and goods were the main traffic, passengers were of secondary consideration. The station, opened in 1836, was thus some distance from the city.
As other companies came into Carlisle in the 1840s, they also used London Road as a terminus. It remained in passenger use until 1 January 1863, when it became a goods depot for the North Eastern Railway, but all was demolished in 1881.

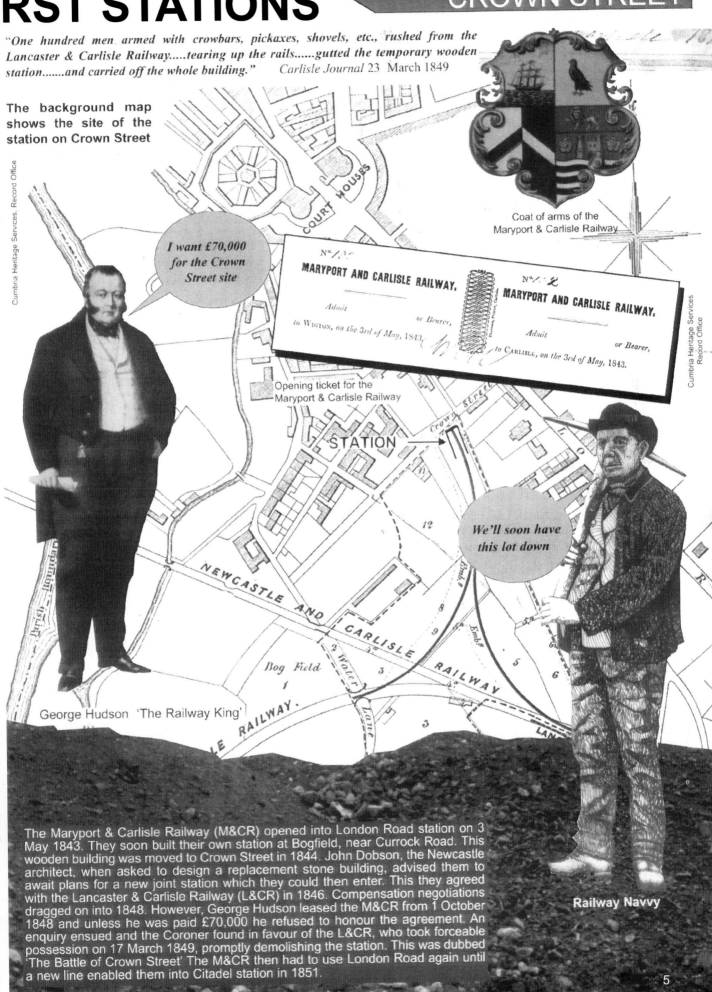

"One hundred men armed with crowbars, pickaxes, shovels, etc., rushed from the Lancaster & Carlisle Railway.....tearing up the rails......gutted the temporary wooden station.......and carried off the whole building." Carlisle Journal 23 March 1849

The background map shows the site of the station on Crown Street

Coat of arms of the Maryport & Carlisle Railway

I want £70,000 for the Crown Street site

Opening ticket for the Maryport & Carlisle Railway

STATION

We'll soon have this lot down

George Hudson 'The Railway King'

Railway Navvy

The Maryport & Carlisle Railway (M&CR) opened into London Road station on 3 May 1843. They soon built their own station at Bogfield, near Currock Road. This wooden building was moved to Crown Street in 1844. John Dobson, the Newcastle architect, when asked to design a replacement stone building, advised them to await plans for a new joint station which they could then enter. This they agreed with the Lancaster & Carlisle Railway (L&CR) in 1846. Compensation negotiations dragged on into 1848. However, George Hudson leased the M&CR from 1 October 1848 and unless he was paid £70,000 he refused to honour the agreement. An enquiry ensued and the Coroner found in favour of the L&CR, who took forceable possession on 17 March 1849, promptly demolishing the station. This was dubbed 'The Battle of Crown Street' The M&CR then had to use London Road again until a new line enabled them into Citadel station in 1851.

5

BUILDING CITADEL STATION

"No less than three hundred men are now employed upon the general station. The underground work having being completed, the foundation stone was laid by Mr R. Hemberow, Architect for the Contractors, on Monday last; the ceremony being followed by three cheers from the assembled workmen, who were afterwards regaled with bread and cheese and beer."
Carlisle Journal 12 March 1847.

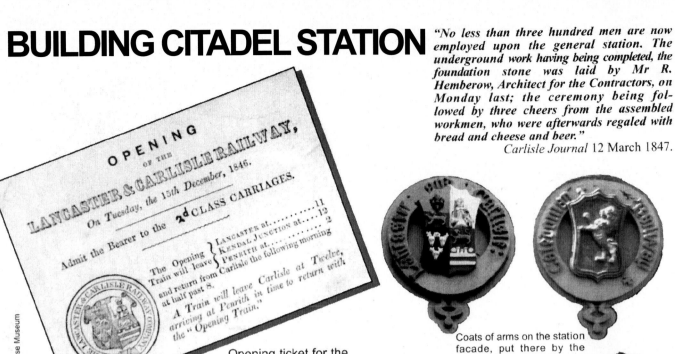

Tullie House Museum

Opening ticket for the Lancaster and Carlisle Railway.

Coats of arms on the station facade, put there by the companies responsible for its construction.

We can build a station to Tite's design for £37,982

Progress is so favourable that I expect it to be completed for use on 15 August 1847

"Many will remember Brown's Row and many other places that have been entirely removed by the railways running into Citadel Station. The removal of these fever nests, as they might be called, was greatly conducive to the health of the people of Carlisle."
Dr R Elliot, 1856

William Tite, architect

Thomas Brassey of Brassey and Stephenson, contractors

The route through Carlisle between England and Scotland was built by two companies - the Lancaster and Carlisle Railway and the Caledonian Railway. It was hoped that the two existing railway companies, the Newcastle and Carlisle, and the Maryport and Carlisle, would use the station and contribute to the costs, but agreement could not be reached.

The Lancaster and Carlisle Railway and the Caledonian Railway formed a committee to oversee the building of a station that they would jointly fund. A site was chosen beside the former Citadel, then converted into courts, and this became the station's name.

Demolition began in 1846 of the gas works and a marble works, which were relocated, along with many slum properties.

Right: Properties which came down to make way for the station.

Map by John Robinson

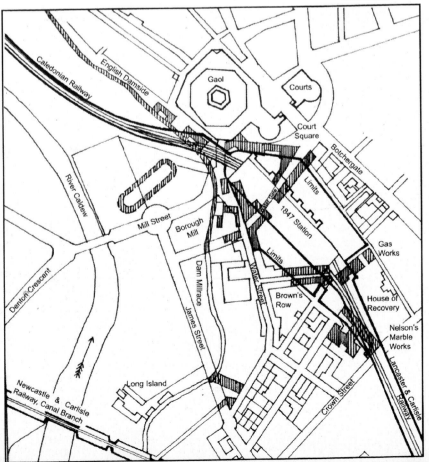

6

RAILWAY EVOLUTION IN CARLISLE

 Became part of

Own station 1836

Maryport and Carlisle.
Own station 1844

 Established joint station 1847  Became part of

Came into station 1863

Came into station 1862

Came into station 1851

Came into station 1851

Came into station 1876

North British + North Eastern became

These 7 companies used the joint station until 1923 when under grouping they became

Glasgow & South Western + Maryport & Carlisle + London & North Western +Caledonian + Midland became

LNER

Which under nationalisation in 1948 became

BRITISH RAILWAYS

LMS

7

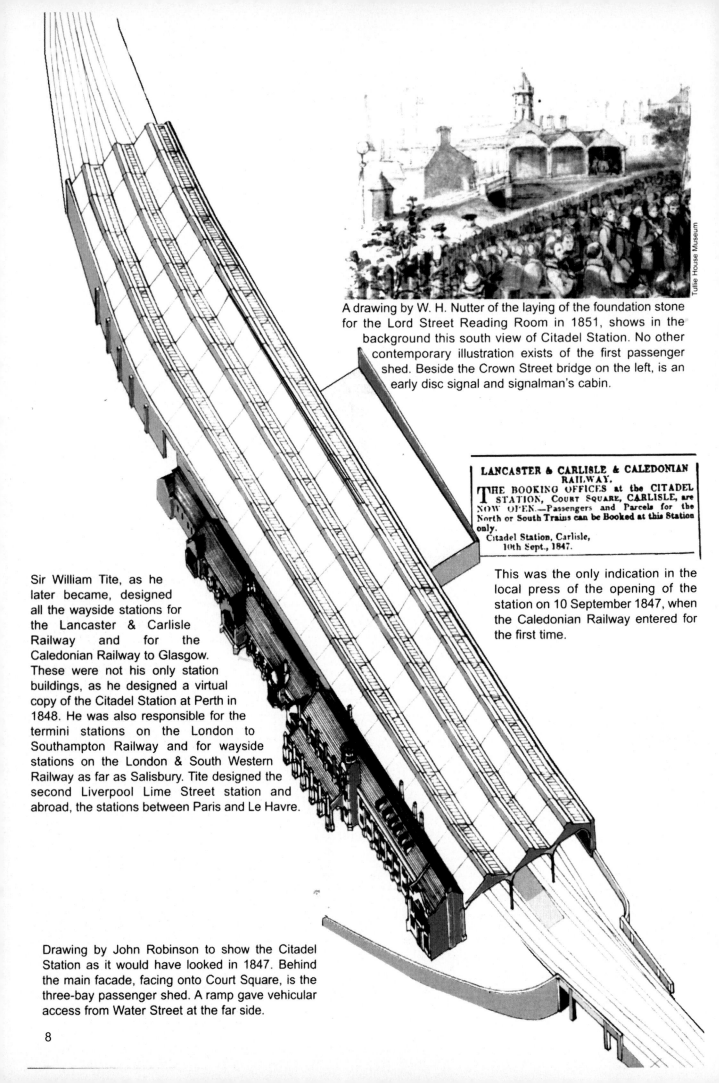

A drawing by W. H. Nutter of the laying of the foundation stone for the Lord Street Reading Room in 1851, shows in the background this south view of Citadel Station. No other contemporary illustration exists of the first passenger shed. Beside the Crown Street bridge on the left, is an early disc signal and signalman's cabin.

LANCASTER & CARLISLE & CALEDONIAN RAILWAY.
THE BOOKING OFFICES at the CITADEL STATION, COURT SQUARE, CARLISLE, are NOW OPEN.—Passengers and Parcels for the North or South Trains can be Booked at this Station only.
Citadel Station, Carlisle,
10th Sept., 1847.

This was the only indication in the local press of the opening of the station on 10 September 1847, when the Caledonian Railway entered for the first time.

Sir William Tite, as he later became, designed all the wayside stations for the Lancaster & Carlisle Railway and for the Caledonian Railway to Glasgow. These were not his only station buildings, as he designed a virtual copy of the Citadel Station at Perth in 1848. He was also responsible for the termini stations on the London to Southampton Railway and for wayside stations on the London & South Western Railway as far as Salisbury. Tite designed the second Liverpool Lime Street station and abroad, the stations between Paris and Le Havre.

Drawing by John Robinson to show the Citadel Station as it would have looked in 1847. Behind the main facade, facing onto Court Square, is the three-bay passenger shed. A ramp gave vehicular access from Water Street at the far side.

CITADEL STATION - 1847

Below: Only part of the facade can be seen from Court Square. Later buildings on the left obscure the view of refreshment and waiting rooms.

"The GENERAL STATION, now in course of erection in Court square,.....will be one of the most extensive and complete buildings of the kind in the empire. The station house, and its appurtenances, will cover an area of several acres, and its style of architecture is to be in the old English or Elizabethan. The front elevation will be 300 feet in length and forty feet in height, with buttresses, and a projecting tower, sixty feet high."

Mannix & Whellan's *Directory of Cumberland*, 1847

Engraving of front elevation - from William Tite's original plans of 1846

Cumbria Heritage Services. Carlisle Library

"The other day we took a turn over the building, and though it is still in an unfinished state, both the exterior and the interior have assumed an elegant and attractive appearance under the skilled hands of Mr Green, who so ably worked on the designs by Mr Tite.......the directors have not neglected a most important item in their catalogue of comforts, namely proper attention to the wants of the inner man......arrangements are going forward in the culinary department, to supply what are soon to become the principal refreshment rooms. A tunnel has been constructed underneath the line for the purpose of communicating with the opposite platform, where there will also be refreshment rooms for the convenience of down passengers."

Carlisle Journal August 1847

'Make us always remember this place, 1848', the Latin inscription on a fireplace in the former first-class refreshment room.

Window in 1847 facade

John Huggon

The interior of the 1847 buildings: the former first class refreshment room in the 1950s. The fireplace shown above is at the end of the room.

With a few modifications, the 1847 station buildings remain much as Tite designed them. It was not until late in1848 that the main facade was completed and it was only on 29 June 1853 that the Joint Station Committee agreed: *"that an illuminated clock be provided for the clock tower."* Costs soared to £53,000.

QUEEN VICTORIA'S VISITS

At half past seven I was woke up to dress and hurry out at Carlisle, which we did at a quarter to eight......there in the station we had some breakfast and waited an hour till our carriage was taken off and another put on......

Opposite inset: Queen Victoria made only one journey on the GSWR, from Carlisle to Renfrew on 22 August 1888. The royal coat-of-arms was applied to the locomotive cabside of No.70, seen in this 1890s view at Carlisle. The arms remained in place for the next twelve years with the hope that the engine would be used to pull a royal train again, but it never did.

Queen Victoria's entry in her Journal for 21 August 1867, after a rather tiresome wait at the Citadel Station. She was later told that changing carriages had been quite unnecessary.

The first class refreshment room where the Queen often stopped on h[er] journeys through Carlisle. In 1851 *"the interior was beautifully s[et] out in readiness for lunch, should her Majesty alight,"* but on th[is] occasion she did not.

Catherine Hepburn

On 30 September 1848, Queen Victoria made her first journey south through Carlisle by rail. She took refreshments at the station and then returned to her carriage. This shows the moment when:-*"the High Sheriff presented to the queen on a silver salver, a beautiful bouquet composed of the gems of Messrs. Little & Ballantyne's greenhouse."* The visit was fully described in the *Carlisle Journal.*

Right: Queen Victoria's royal train in Carlisle in 1897. Caledonian locomotives which were to take the train north, had been specially named *Jubilee* and *Victoria* to celebrate her Diamond Jubilee.
Painting by C Hamilton Ellis.

Citadel Railway Station, Carlisle.

Her Majesty's Journey from Ballater to Windsor.
On Thursday, 15th November, 1888.

"The Royal Train to arrive, at Carlisle, on Thursday, 15th November, at 11-30 p.m., and leave at 11-50 p.m.

None of the Public are on this occasion, under any circumstances, to be admitted to the Station. The Servants are to perform the necessary work on the Platform without noise; no cheering or other demonstration must be allowed—the object being that Her Majesty shall be perfectly undisturbed. The Station to be kept clear and private.

The London and North Western Guards to be in readiness at the front and rear vans to exchange with the Caledonian Guards, who must not pass along the Platform until after the departure of the Royal Train.

By Order,
JOHN THOMSON,
Secretary.

Citadel Station, Carlisle, 14th November, 1888.

As this poster shows, such viewing of the Queen was later discouraged.

"The platform had seats in semicircles crowded with ladies, many the most respectable citizens..... a guard from the Castle was behind them at the south end. On the west side was a crowd of the working classes, whose orderly conduct was of general remark ...... between 1500 and 2000 were within the station. A discharge of cannon from the Castle announced arrival .... the band struck up and the Royal carriages, drawn by two engines, entered amidst loud and long continued cheering ..... as the train stopped her Majesty rose, opened the window and graciously bowed in acknowledgement. Prince Albert, the Prince of Wales and the Princess Royal stood forward to gaze upon the gay scene. The Mayor presented the Address but the cheering was so loud that it was impossible to hear. The ladies on the front seats first stood upon the forms ...... then, many rushed forward to get a clearer sight ..... policemen and others tried to stem the tide, till at last the military advanced .... this movement had the desired effect. It was the first time the military had been called to put down a mob of ladies."

Carlisle Journal, 10 October 1851

EARLY EXTENSIONS

Drawing by John Robinson to show the station as enlarged in 1862. Compare this with the illustrations on page 6 and that on page 18.

"Lord Palmerston took the arm of Mr Jones, secretary to the Joint Station Committee when he got out of the train and spent most of the quarter of an hour during which the train stopped in promenading the platform........ the Premier observing the progress of the works of Borough Street Bridge, remarked upon the convenience of the station and jocularly suggested ..... it would make a capital rifle range....."

Carlisle Journal 7 April 1863.

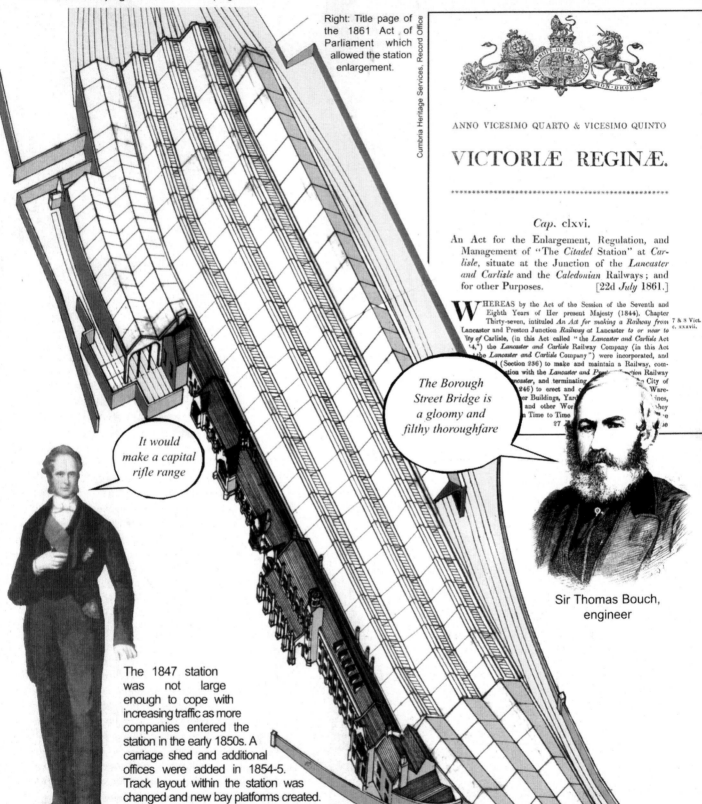

Right: Title page of the 1861 Act of Parliament which allowed the station enlargement.

Cumbria Heritage Services. Record Office

ANNO VICESIMO QUARTO & VICESIMO QUINTO

VICTORIÆ REGINÆ.

Cap. clxvi.

An Act for the Enlargement, Regulation, and Management of "The *Citadel* Station" at *Carlisle*, situate at the Junction of the *Lancaster and Carlisle* and the *Caledonian* Railways; and for other Purposes. [22d *July* 1861.]

WHEREAS by the Act of the Session of the Seventh and Eighth Years of Her present Majesty (1844). Chapter Thirty-seven, intituled *An Act for making a Railway from* 7 & 8 Vict. *Lancaster* and Preston Junction *Railway* at Lancaster *to or near to* c. xxxvii. *'ity of* Carlisle, (in this Act called " the *Lancaster and Carlisle* Act '4,") the *Lancaster and Carlisle* Railway Company (in this Act the *Lancaster and Carlisle* Company ") were incorporated, and d (Section 236) to make and maintain a Railway, com-tion with the *Lancaster and P* tion Railway *ncaster*, and terminating City of 246) to erect and Ware-er Buildings, Yard ines, and other Wor hey n Time to Time 27

It would make a capital rifle range

The Borough Street Bridge is a gloomy and filthy thoroughfare

Sir Thomas Bouch, engineer

The 1847 station was not large enough to cope with increasing traffic as more companies entered the station in the early 1850s. A carriage shed and additional offices were added in 1854-5. Track layout within the station was changed and new bay platforms created. When the Joint Committee sought powers to enlarge the station in 1861 the plans were opposed by the City Council, who objected to the bridges at either end of the approaches. Thomas Bouch was engaged to advise the city, but their objections failed to impede the progress of the Bill through Parliament. It was the subsequent work to widen Borough Street Bridge that Lord Palmerston saw on his visit in 1863.

Lord Palmerston

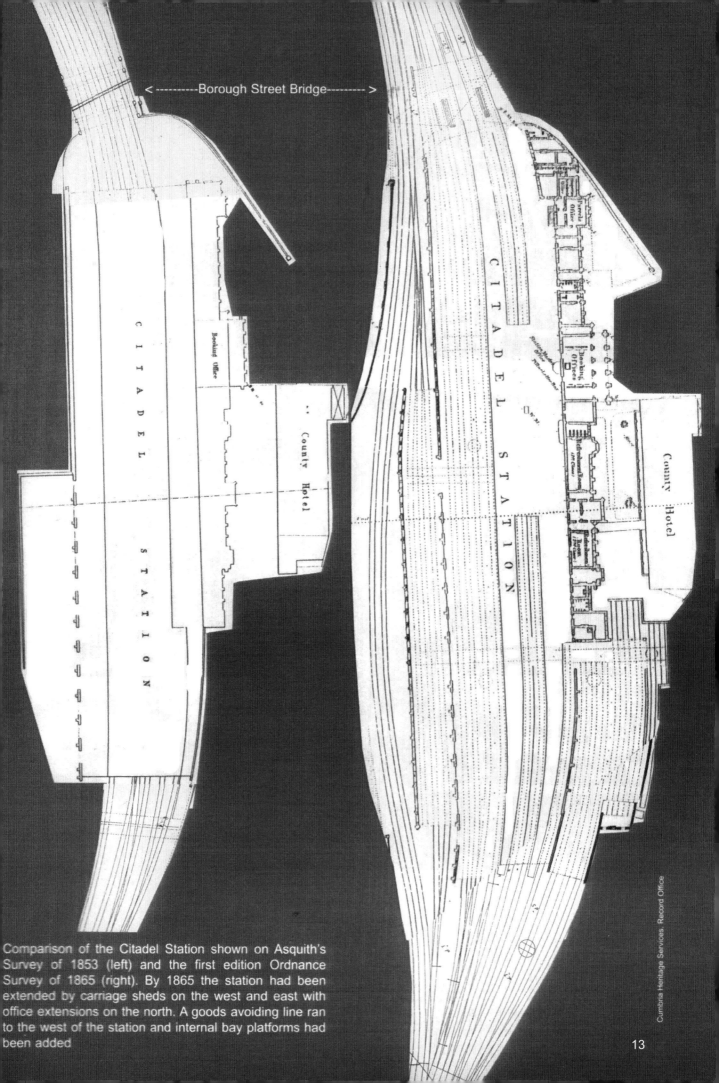

<----------Borough Street Bridge---------->

CITADEL STATION

Booking Office

County Hotel

CITADEL STATION

County Hotel

Comparison of the Citadel Station shown on Asquith's Survey of 1853 (left) and the first edition Ordnance Survey of 1865 (right). By 1865 the station had been extended by carriage sheds on the west and east with office extensions on the north. A goods avoiding line ran to the west of the station and internal bay platforms had been added

13

A RAILWAY CENTRE

CALEDONIAN RAILWAY

NORTH BRITISH RAILWAY

GLASGOW & SOUTH WESTERN RLY.

NORTH EASTERN RAILWAY

MARYPORT & CARLISLE RAILWAY

MIDLAND RAILWAY

LONDON & NORTH WESTERN RAILWAY

Locomotives in Carlisle of each of the seven railway companies using the station.

CONTRABAND

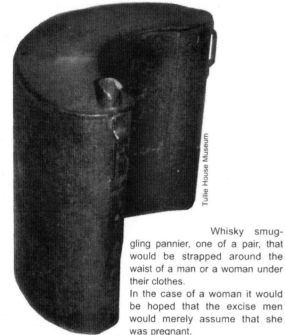

Tullie House Museum

Whisky smuggling pannier, one of a pair, that would be strapped around the waist of a man or a woman under their clothes.

In the case of a woman it would be hoped that the excise men would merely assume that she was pregnant.

In 1830 the duty on spirits in Scotland was 3s 4d per proof gallon and in England 7s 6d; this difference in duty created a lucrative trade in the smuggling of spirits across the border. This resulted in excise officers attending at Berwick and Carlisle railway stations for the examination of passengers' baggage.

This new form of border control caused considerable public interest, especially in letters to *The Times*, where there was concern that the country was becoming "*a minor European principality with annoying and petty border restrictions.*" This however, was not to last for long; the Spirit Duty in both countries was equalised, so the Border Service ceased on 18 September 1855.

Public Record Office / BTC H R. P(5) 1/40

BY AUTHORITY.

PUBLIC NOTICE.

The **PUBLIC** are requested to take Notice, that the Transmission of all **FOREIGN** and **COLONIAL SPIRITS** between Scotland and England, by Land, is contrary to Law.

Spirits Distilled in Scotland can only be transmitted, by Land, in quantities exceeding Twenty Gallons, accompanied by an Excise Permit; the full rate of English Duty having been previously paid.

All Scotch Spirits found in Transit, per the Caledonian Railway, in less quantities than Twenty Gallons, and all such Spirits of that or any greater quantity unaccompanied by the necessary Permit, are liable to be seized by the Officers of the Excise.

The Caledonian Railway Company refuse to undertake the Conveyance of Spirits, except when the conditions of the Excise Regulations have been complied with, and when they are supplied with the Name and Address both of the party sending and the party to receive the Consignment.

All Packages containing Liquids of any description are liable to detention, on suspicion; to avoid which, it is desirable their contents should be stated at the time of Booking.

By order,

J. W. CODDINGTON, Secy.

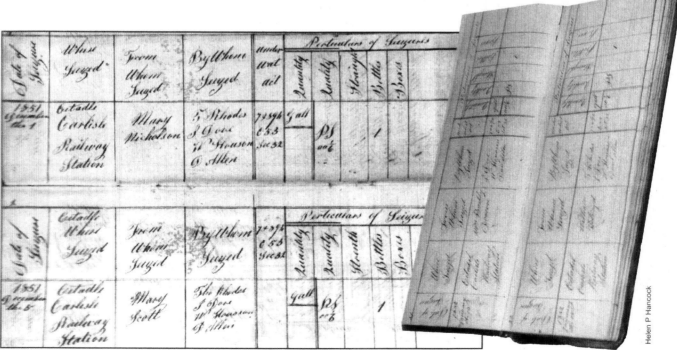

Helen P Hancock

Customs book kept by Daniel Allen. The page shown gives details of the seizure of bottles of spirits at Citadel Station from Mary Nicholson and Mary Scott on 1 and 5 December 1851.

COUNTY HOTEL AND REFRESHMENT ROOMS

"No visitor will resist the temptation of taking up his quarters, whether temporarily or for a prolonged stay, at the best of hostelries in Carlisle, 'The County.' For comfort and space, this fine building is not eclipsed by any provincial hotel -- having 120 rooms, and a retinue of forty servants."
Illustrated guide to the Lancaster & Carlisle and Caledonian Railways, 1859

B.B.Breach
Joint Station Refreshment Rooms
AND
BUSH FAMILY HOTEL.
CARLISLE.
This Hotel is the nearest to the Ra...
and opposite the P...

B.B.Breach
COUNTY HOTEL
AND
Refreshment Rooms
CARLISLE.
The Hotel is FIRE PROOF & is approached from the Station Platform by a covered way
Attendance charged in the Bill
Nº 1828   3/29.54

Cumbria Heritage Services, Carlisle Library

Behind me is the covered passage to the hotel

Maurice Bell

Awaiting the arrival of Princess Margaret, 1951

Cream jug from the refreshment rooms

Land in Court Square not required for station building was leased to George Head Head, but only on condition he built a station hotel.

Anthony Salvin, a leading architect who worked on Windsor Castle, designed the hotel with a suite of royal apartments intended for Queen Victoria to break her journey to and from Balmoral. A covered way linked with the station platforms. Work was completed in 1853 for a visit of the Queen for a meal, accompanied by Prince Albert and the Prince of Wales. But she did not stay and never did.

Mr Breach, formerly of the Bush, took the new hotel and he had won the contract for running the station refreshment rooms. Complaints about the standards in 1916 caused the hotel to lose the franchise and the refreshment rooms were then run by the Caledonian Railway and its successors.

On Victoria's visit to the hotel in 1853 the *Carlisle Patriot* reported:

"The Queen was very cheerful and affable and took a great interest in everything around her and the Prince Consort gazed around him with evident pleasure. She examined all the pictures on the stairs and drew the Prince's attention to a fine antique clock. While passing along the Queen turned to the Prince of Wales and said:"

This is the new hotel my dear

George Head
Head's initials

The date above
a window

1852

Engraving of County Hotel, 1859

VICTORIA VIADUCT

Princess Louise

I have much pleasure in declaring this viaduct open.

Victoria Viaduct in November 1898 from the Electric Lighting Station chimney.

When the Midland Railway came into Carlisle in 1876 it was necessary to radically rethink access to the Citadel Station. Goods traffic was re-routed to by-pass the station on a new line through Denton Holme and the approaches to the station from the north and south were completely rebuilt. Borough Street bridge, which had formerly taken the road to Denton Holme under the north end of the station, was abandoned in favour of a new high level viaduct which crossed both the station and goods line. This was named after Queen Victoria and her daughter, Louise, came to open it in 1877. Without these improvements the station could not have been enlarged in 1880.

VICTORIA VIADUCT
OPENED BY
HER ROYAL HIGHNESS THE PRINCESS LOUISE
20TH SEPTEMBER 1877
COMMENCED 1876
JOSEPH BENDLE ESQUIRE MAYOR
COMPLETED 1877
SAMUEL JACKSON BINNING ESQUIRE MAYOR

The foundation stone of Shap Granite

Princess Louise opening the Viaduct, 20 September 1877

1880 EXTENSIONS

The station showing the full extent of the south screen and the west wall

The Citadel Station could not cope with proposed increases of traffic and in 1871 the Joint Committee sought the necessary powers to purchase land for additions. The division of goods and passenger lines relieved some of the congestion caused by the introduction of the Midland Railway in 1876.

Initial work began in 1878 to enlarge the station to almost twice its original size with an overall roof. Impressive timber glazed screens in Gothic style formed the north and south elevations, with a massive west wall to support the roof. New island platforms with connecting footbridges, had buildings which provided additional refreshment rooms waiting rooms and offices. All was completed by 1881.

Cumbria Heritage Services, Carlisle Library

British Railways Board/Railtrack PLC

CARLISLE CITADEL STATION

PLANS & SECTIONS.

November 1871.

Architect's design for the south screen, as built.

Public Record Office

18

ER 950 simmers outside the station at the turn of the century. The south screen
f the roof forms the backdrop.

the 1930s Davidson's Garage was under the arches of the west side of the
ation. Margaretta Davidson is in the foreground and her husband, Jack
avidson, whose garage it was, is the fourth from the right.

1950s view of what remained of South John Street, showing damage to the
ass at the west side of the station roof.

e south-west angle of the station shows in the background of this 1909 view
the Crown Street coal depot of the Maryport & Carlisle Railway.

Citadel Station at its full extent, shown on the 1900 OS
map. This gives the ground floor use of each room in the
station. Compare this with earlier maps on page 11.

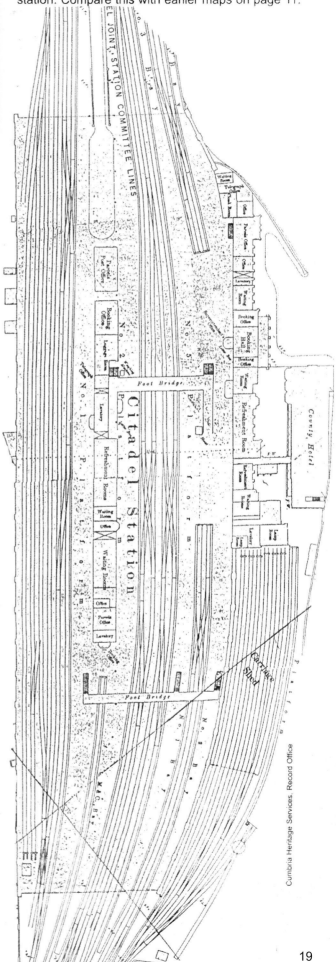

19

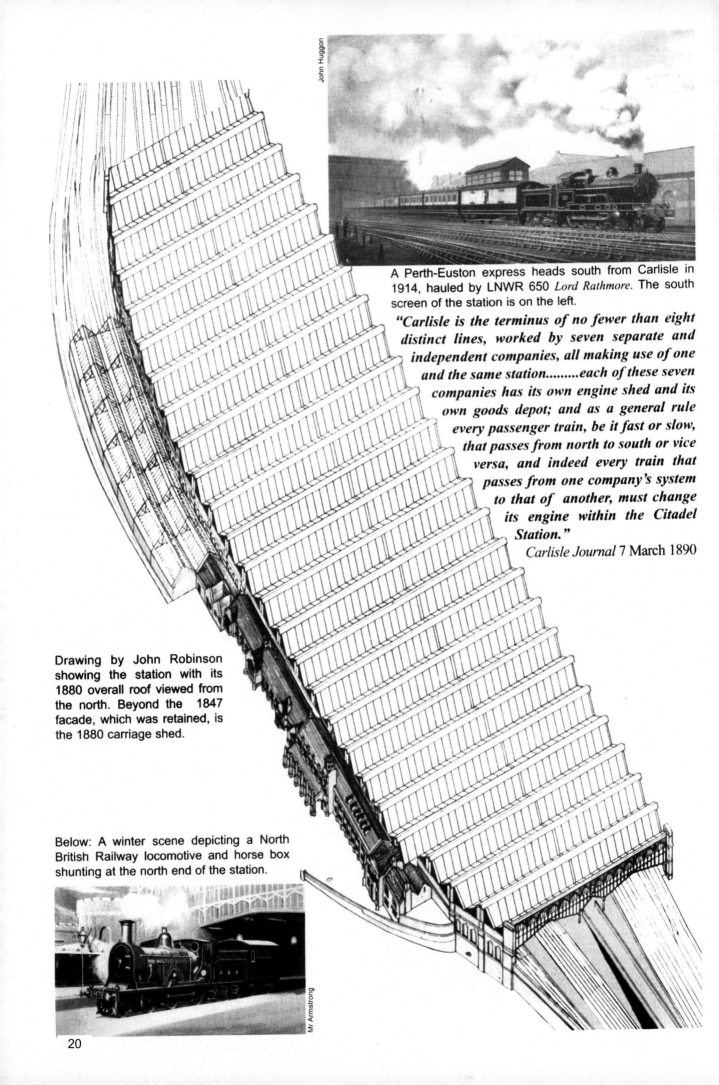

John Huggon

A Perth-Euston express heads south from Carlisle in 1914, hauled by LNWR 650 *Lord Rathmore*. The south screen of the station is on the left.

"Carlisle is the terminus of no fewer than eight distinct lines, worked by seven separate and independent companies, all making use of one and the same station.........each of these seven companies has its own engine shed and its own goods depot; and as a general rule every passenger train, be it fast or slow, that passes from north to south or vice versa, and indeed every train that passes from one company's system to that of another, must change its engine within the Citadel Station."

Carlisle Journal 7 March 1890

Drawing by John Robinson showing the station with its 1880 overall roof viewed from the north. Beyond the 1847 facade, which was retained, is the 1880 carriage shed.

Below: A winter scene depicting a North British Railway locomotive and horse box shunting at the north end of the station.

Mr Armstrong

1880 BUILDINGS

Ironwork from the 1880 roof survives today

Granite drinking fountains of 1880 can be seen on platforms 1 and 3

Right: Many of the 1880 island buildings facing platforms 1 and 3 retain original linen-fold panelled doors and etched glass windows.

Agreement had been reached in 1872 with the Midland Railway that, when their line from Settle was completed, they would have to pay the costs of the station extension to accommodate them. The Midland Railway argued that the estimated costs of £155,901 19s 6d were excessive, but still had to pay.

William Edgecumbe Rendle, horticulturist turned architect, used his "Invincible" patent in the roof design. The contractors for the main building work were the Glasgow firm of Morrison & Mason and the roof was by Messrs Arrol, also of Glasgow, who went on to build the Forth Bridge.

Work began in October 1878, but the severe winter held up progress. The Joint Station Committee were anxious to have the work completed by July 1880 because traffic would be heavy for the Royal Show; which was being held in Carlisle. The island buildings were far from being finished when the footbridge was in use for the first time on 4 July 1880, but the station coped with the show influx the following weekend. It was not until 20 July 1881 that the new refreshment rooms opened; which marked the end of reconstruction work.

This photograph shows the overall roof and in the foreground is the second footbridge which linked the southern bay platforms until its removal in 1942. The overhead smokeplates, installed in 1883, deflected engine smoke to prevent soot rising directly to the glass roof.

Peter W Robinson

CARLISLE CITADEL JOINT STATION COMMITTEE

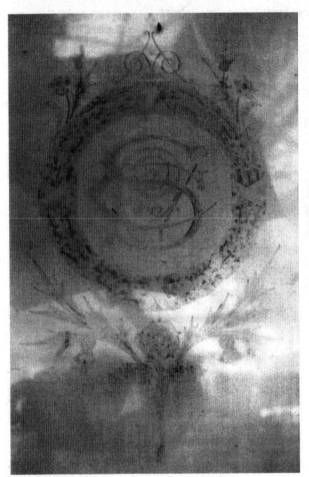

"Might I call the attention of the public... to a nuisance which seems peculiar to Carlisle - I mean the loud and apparently unnecessary whistling of the engines in the Citadel Station....people who are afflicted with weak nerves and the public generally I am sure would be glad if anything could be done to remedy or at least lessen this evil."

A complaint of 1873 to the Joint Committee made by a traveller.

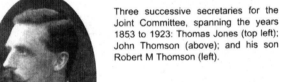

Three successive secretaries for the Joint Committee, spanning the years 1853 to 1923: Thomas Jones (top left); John Thomson (above); and his son Robert M Thomson (left).

The only surviving etched glass window (there had been four) in the 1880 refreshment room, showing the monogram CCSC of the Joint Committee.

From the beginning the station was run by a Joint Committee of representatives from the two companies that had built it; the Caledonian and Lancaster & Carlisle Railways. As other companies entered the station they did so as tenants paying an annual rental, but had no say in the running of the station. S. E. Bolden of the L & C Railway was the first secretary of the committee. He was replaced by Thomas Jones in 1853, when he also became Station Superintendent. There were only two further long serving secretaries until grouping in 1923 when the LMS took responsibility for the station and the Committee was abolished.

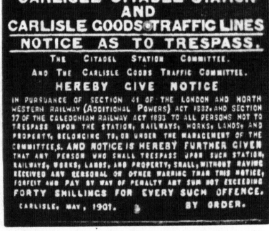

Above: Each bridge and subway in the station carried a number plate with the Joint Committee initials.
Right: Trespass notices were also issued by the Joint Committee

SUPERINTENDENTS, MASTERS & MANAGERS

Railway Magazine Nov 1900

"Stationmaster will have a peaked cap or a bowler hat instead of the old top hat....we don't know whether the top hat will go for good, but I think it's a bit archaic.... I don't think we want it on British Railways.... the main uniform for stationmasters will be a well-cut civilian suit." George Williams, Chief Design Officer, British Railways Board, February 1963.

William Haythornthwaite surveys his domain in an unusually empty station. He was Superintendent between 1897-1910 and came from the same position at Carnforth. The inset shows him in 1900. He had to retire through ill-health at the early age of 59.

A Superintendent was appointed to oversee the smooth running of the station. Top hat and frock coat was the everyday uniform, which later became topper and tails. Passengers would see him in full uniform to greet crack expresses.

At first the Superintendent lived above the entrance to the station, but later he had a house in the city.

In the 1930s his title changed to Station Master, but the uniform was retained until 1952 and then re-introduced in 1955.

Due to the change of image with the creation of the British Railways Board in 1963, new uniforms were adopted. Job titles changed and in 1966 the position of Station Master was abolished to be replaced by an Area Manager.

Above: At special times after 1963, James Leslie, Station Master from 1958-1966, wore top hat and tails. He stands here on platform 4 for the last time on his retirement in 1966.

Right: In 1986 Sarah Kendall became Station Manager, the first time a woman was appointed to such a position in the country.

Further illustrations of Station Superintendents / Masters will be found on other pages and a list on page 51.

Don Mc Phee / The Guardian, 13 September 1986

STATION STAFF

"That station staff of 230 including eight inspectors, six foremen and 18 signalmen, under Mr Campbell, the Superintendent, assisted by Mr Bell, the Night Superintendent, owe their success in a large measure to their familiarity with technicalities of train working, to their local knowledge, length of service, and urbanity, for it has become a byeword in distant parts of the world that the Carlisle officials and porters are the most polite and considerate to be found anywhere."

Carlisle Journal, 16 August 1910

Alistair Leslie

Nicol Campbell, Station Superintendent in top hat, poses with a group of Citadel Station staff in Court Square gardens before World War I. There is no photograph which shows the entire staff.

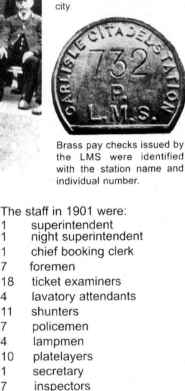

Citadel Station uniform button. These came in two sizes and had a silvered finish. The coat of arms was that of the city.

Brass pay checks issued by the LMS were identified with the station name and individual number.

Ashley Kendall / J Allan Simms

INSPECTOR   **PORTER**   **LAMPMAN**   **TICKET EXAMINER**

The staff in 1901 were:

1	superintendent
1	night superintendent
1	chief booking clerk
7	foremen
18	ticket examiners
4	lavatory attendants
11	shunters
7	policemen
4	lampmen
10	platelayers
1	secretary
7	inspectors
9	booking clerks
1	parcel clerks
20	signalmen
4	luggage room attendants
8	ladies room attendants
6	shacklers
36	porters
2	enginemen
8	painters, joiners, plumbers etc.

The Citadel Joint Station Committee agreed at a meeting on 17 August 1847 that their staff of superintendent, booking clerk, parcel clerk and six porters, should be increased on the opening of the station. A check taker was to be appointed; two more porters, three policemen, two pointsmen and a woman to attend on ladies and clean. Staff uniform was to be the same as the LNWR with the initials CJS for 'Citadel Joint Station' and number on the collar. By 1901 there were 182 employees in the station, which by 1910, had risen to 230. This did not include the refreshment rooms staff. Uniforms signified different jobs, but in a group photograph it is difficult to identify individual roles. The superintendent always stands out in top hat and policemen with high collars and pillbox hats. Gold bands on hats signified rank, as did a frock coat. By 1900 the committee had shortened the uniform initials to CS. From 1923 LMS uniform was adopted.

THE STATION AT WORK

A porter tends the fire in the first class waiting room in November 1934

Carlisle Journal 27 November 1934

Refreshment room staff prepare British Railways sandwiches in the 1950s.

John Huggon

IN A SIGNAL CABIN AT CARLISLE STATION

At busy times in the summer, here in June 1935, youths were employed to sell chocolate and sweets from trays, along the station platforms.

Carlisle Journal 5 July 1935

Carlisle Journal 12 July 1935

Above: Signalmen Crosthwaite and Hutton are pulling levers on 8 July 1935 in No 5 signal box, at the south end of the station.

Below: porters hurry along the platform with luggage and parcels for a southbound LNWR train at sometime before 1910.

Once a person was in a station job it was often a job for life. To illustrate here are two examples: Mrs Booth retired in 1912 after 50 years service. She attended ladies in the same waiting room, on what was then platform 5. Robert Errington, who retired in 1945, could remember rolling out the red carpet for Queen Victoria in 1899.

NEWSPAPER STANDS

This 1904 photograph shows Nicol Campbell, the Night Superintendent in full uniform of top hat and frock coat, beside Menzies stall which was against the footbridge ramp of what is today platform 3.

A Menzies newsboy with basket, posed beside a southbound express about 1910. He would sell newspapers to passengers through carriage windows.

James Arthur, a Carlisle bookseller and publisher, secured the contract for the sale of newspapers at Citadel Station on 11 December 1848, at an annual rent of £5. This franchise was periodically renewed at a revised rental and in 1855 the sum rose to £20.

Joint Station Committee minutes show that Mr Arthur negotiated a ten-year contract on 28 July 1859 for £52 per annum. When the cost was again to rise at the end of the period, he decided to retire and John Menzies, who had bookstalls on most Scottish stations, took his place.

As these photographs show, John Menzies stalls have moved around the station with kiosks on the main platforms.

William Haythornthwaite, Station Superintendent, stands prominently in top hat and frock coat in this 1900 view of Menzies stall near the station entrance.

This 1904 view shows Menzies stall close to the footbridge, facing what is today platform 4.

Menzies stall was still under the footbridge ramp when this view was taken in 1953 of the Coronation decorations. This stall faced the refreshment rooms, close to the entrance onto platform 4.

TRAFFIC

"Saturday, two days before the King made his first journey through Carlisle since his accession, no fewer than 91 trains ran which do not appear in the timetables, making the total number of trains on that day alone 361, which is believed to be a record." Carlisle Journal, 16th August 1910.

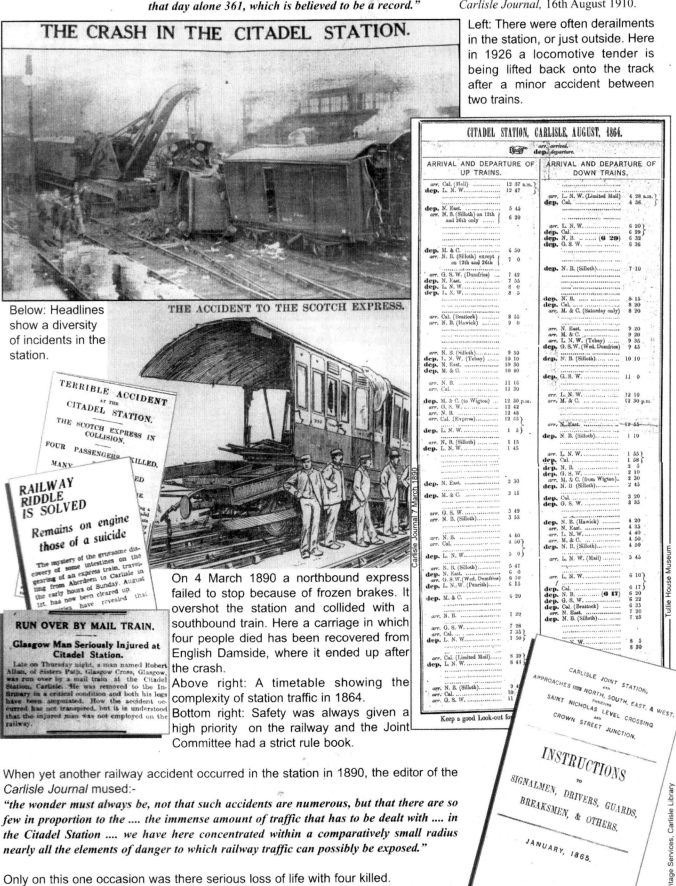

THE CRASH IN THE CITADEL STATION.

Carlisle Journal 24 September 1926

Left: There were often derailments in the station, or just outside. Here in 1926 a locomotive tender is being lifted back onto the track after a minor accident between two trains.

Below: Headlines show a diversity of incidents in the station.

THE ACCIDENT TO THE SCOTCH EXPRESS.

Carlisle Journal 7 March 1890

TERRIBLE ACCIDENT AT THE CITADEL STATION.
THE SCOTCH EXPRESS IN COLLISION.
FOUR PASSENGERS KILLED.
MANY ...
Carlisle Journal 7 March 1890

RAILWAY RIDDLE IS SOLVED
Remains on engine those of a suicide
The mystery of the gruesome discovery of some intestines on the gearing of an express train, travelling from Aberdeen to Carlisle in the early hours of Sunday, August 1st, has now been cleared up. ... have revealed that ...
CEN 17 August 1948

RUN OVER BY MAIL TRAIN.
Glasgow Man Seriously Injured at Citadel Station.
Late on Thursday night, a man named Robert Allan, of Sisters Path, Glasgow Cross, Glasgow, was run over by a mail train at the Citadel Station, Carlisle. He was removed to the Infirmary in a critical condition and both his legs have been amputated. How the accident occurred has not transpired, but it is understood that the injured man was not employed on the railway.
CJ 14 March 1922

On 4 March 1890 a northbound express failed to stop because of frozen brakes. It overshot the station and collided with a southbound train. Here a carriage in which four people died has been recovered from English Damside, where it ended up after the crash.

Above right: A timetable showing the complexity of station traffic in 1864.

Bottom right: Safety was always given a high priority on the railway and the Joint Committee had a strict rule book.

CITADEL STATION, CARLISLE, AUGUST, 1864.

arr. arrival. dep. departure.

ARRIVAL AND DEPARTURE OF UP TRAINS.		ARRIVAL AND DEPARTURE OF DOWN TRAINS.	
arr. Cal. (Mail)	12 37 a.m.		
dep. L. N. W.	12 47		
		arr. L. N. W. (Limited Mail)	4 28 a.m.
		dep. Cal.	4 36
dep. N. East.	5 45		
arr. N. B. (Silloth) on 12th and 26th only	6 20		
		arr. L. N. W.	6 20
		dep. Cal.	6 29
		dep. N. B. (6 29)	6 32
		dep. G. S. W.	6 36
dep. M. & C.	6 50		
arr. N. B. (Silloth) except on 12th and 26th	7 0		
		dep. N. B. (Silloth)	7 10
arr. G. S. W. (Dumfries)	7 42		
dep. N. East.	7 55		
dep. L. N. W.	8 0		
dep. L. N. W.	8 5		
		dep. N. B.	8 15
		dep. Cal.	8 20
		arr. M. & C. (Saturday only)	8 20
arr. Cal. (Beattock)	8 55		
arr. N. B. (Hawick)	9 0		
		arr. N. East.	9 20
		arr. M. & C.	9 20
		arr. L. N. W. (Tebay)	9 35
		dep. G. S. W. (Wed. Dumfries)	9 45
arr. N. B. (Silloth)	9 50		
dep. L. N. W. (Tebay)	10 10	dep. N. B. (Silloth)	10 10
dep. N. East.	10 30		
dep. M. & C.	10 40		
arr. N. B.	11 16	dep. G. S. W.	11 0
arr. Cal.	11 30		
		arr. L. N. W.	12 10
dep. M. & C. (to Wigton)	12 30 p.m.	arr. M. & C.	12 30 p.m.
dep. G. S. W.	12 42		
dep. N. B.	12 48		
arr. Cal. (Express)	12 53		
		arr. N. East.	12 55
dep. L. N. W.	1 5	dep. N. B. (Silloth)	1 10
arr. N. B. (Silloth)	1 15		
dep. L. N. W.	1 45		
		arr. L. N. W.	1 55
		dep. Cal.	1 58
		dep. N. B.	2 5
		dep. G. S. W.	2 10
		arr. M. & C. (from Wigton)	2 30
dep. N. East.	2 30	dep. N. B (Silloth)	2 45
dep. M. & C.	3 15		
		dep. Cal.	3 20
		dep. G. S. W.	3 35
arr. G. S. W.	3 49		
arr. N. B. (Silloth)	3 53		
		dep. N. B. (Hawick)	4 20
		arr. N. East.	4 35
arr. N. B.	4 40	arr. L. N. W.	4 40
arr. Cal.	4 50	arr. M. & C.	4 50
		dep. N. B. (Silloth)	4 50
dep. L. N. W.	5 0		
		arr. L. N. W. (Mail)	5 45
arr. N. B. (Silloth)	5 47		
dep. N. East.	6 0		
arr. G. S. W. (Wed. Dumfries)	6 10	arr. L. N. W.	6 10
dep. L. N. W. (Penrith)	6 15	dep. Cal.	6 17
		dep. N. B. (6 17)	6 20
dep. M. & C.	6 20	dep. G. S. W.	6 22
		dep. Cal. (Beattock)	6 35
		arr. N. East.	7 20
arr. N. B.	7 20	dep. N. B. (Silloth)	7 25
arr. G. S. W.	7 28		
arr. Cal.	7 35		
dep. L. N. W.	7 50		
		...W.	8 5
			8 30
arr. Cal. (Limited Mail)	8 39		
dep. L. N. W.	8 44		
arr. N. B. (Silloth)	9 4...		
arr. Cal.	9...		
arr. G. S. W.	11 ...		

Keep a good Look-out for ...

Tullie House Museum.

CARLISLE JOINT STATION, AND APPROACHES FROM NORTH, SOUTH, EAST, & WEST, INCLUDING SAINT NICHOLAS LEVEL CROSSING AND CROWN STREET JUNCTION.

INSTRUCTIONS TO SIGNALMEN, DRIVERS, GUARDS, BREAKSMEN, & OTHERS.

JANUARY, 1865.

Cumbria Heritage Services, Carlisle Library

When yet another railway accident occurred in the station in 1890, the editor of the *Carlisle Journal* mused:-

"the wonder must always be, not that such accidents are numerous, but that there are so few in proportion to the .... the immense amount of traffic that has to be dealt with .... in the Citadel Station .... we have here concentrated within a comparatively small radius nearly all the elements of danger to which railway traffic can possibly be exposed."

Only on this one occasion was there serious loss of life with four killed.
There were other accidents which resulted in loss of life and amputations, but this was often caused by drunken passengers falling off platforms under passing trains, rather than staff neglect.

27

ROYAL VISITS

Right: Royal train notices were issued giving instructions to staff.

LONDON AND NORTH WESTERN RAILWAY.

LOCAL INSTRUCTIONS FOR WORKING THE

ROYAL TRAIN

FROM

CARLISLE to LONDON (Euston),

On MONDAY, the 10th OCTOBER, 1904.

1. EVERY PERSON S...
   IN HIS POSS...
   (BLUE NOT...

2. The time of
   telegraphed
   telegraphed

3. A Pilot

The arrival of Princess Louise on 24 September 1908. She was on a visit to the Cumberland Infirmary. The Earl of Lonsdale greeted her with his own carriage in front of a guard of honour.

Princess Anne leaving the station on 27 April 1972 on an official visit to the city

Every British monarch since the station was built has passed through Carlisle at regular intervals, but they did not always stop.

Foreign royalty also occasionally stretched their legs in Carlisle on long journeys but, as rail travel improved and travel times were reduced, this became less common.

For the present Queen's official visit to Carlisle in 1958 the station was lavishly decorated but, as she was taken ill at the last minute, she never saw these. All had been taken down when she finally came later in the year.

Other members of the Royal Family have made official visits to Carlisle in recent years and have often travelled by rail.

Queen Elizabeth II on 16 October 1958

Princess Margaret reviews a guard of honour outside the station after arriving for an official visit on 8 August 1951. Lord Lieutenant Sir Robert Chance and Mayor, Alderman G H Routledge are also on the podium.

Left: The Duchess of York arrived by Royal train to open the new facilities at Carlisle Station on 7 April 1989. Here the Lord Lieutenant, Sir Charles Graham introduces the High Sheriff, and his wife, Tarn Riley.

George V and Queen Mary gree... Queen Wilhelmina of th... Netherlands at Carlisle Statio... where they took refreshmen... together before the King an... Queen continued their journey ... Edinburgh on 9 July 1923.

FAMOUS VISITORS

MR. LLOYD GEORGE SPEAKING FROM THE ROYAL SCOT.

Cumbria Heritage Services, Carlisle Library

Carlisle Journal 17 April 1928

Lloyd George drew large crowds to the station when he passed through, long after his term as Prime Minister.

A *Punch* cartoon of Gladstone leaving Carlisle in 1879, before he had finished his speech. As Prime Minister he often spoke to crowds in the station when passing through.

Notice for the visit of the Khan of Afghanistan in 1895. He was to go on to see guns being tested at Silloth.

NOBLE ROMAN' VISITS CARLISLE

Cumberland News

Charlton Heston stands outside the station on a 1960s visit to the area.

"Have a Go" Pickles comes to Wetheral

Cumberland Evening News 29 October 1962

Wilfred Pickles came to Carlisle in 1962 to present his radio programme *"Have a Go"* from Wetheral. He is greeted by James Leslie, the Station Master. Millions of people listened to his broadcasts each week.

Prior to 1960 few people would consider making a long journey by road or air in Britain. Everyone travelled by train. Prime Ministers, generals, presidents, stars of film, radio and television, and many others, passed through the station. Sometimes they paused on their journeys and it was traditional that Prime Ministers would make a brief speech.

Below: President Woodrow Wilson boards his train for Manchester after a visit to his mother's birthplace in Carlisle in December 1918.

Railway Magazine, February 1919

World War II hero Field Marshal Montgomery leaves the station in his wartime campaign car, together with Mayor, Harold Greenop, on 17 May 1947. He came to be given the freedom of the City of Carlisle.

City of Carlisle

STRIKES

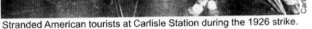

Strike breakers in 1926 were afterwards awarded a bronze medal by the LMS. This was presented to driver William Hodgson of Edentown

Tullie House Museum

Stranded American tourists at Carlisle Station during the 1926 strike.

Carlisle Journal 7 May 1926

Volunteers moving essential supplies, load milk for Newcastle in the 1926 strike.

Carlisle Journal 7 May 1926

In 1926 union members came together in Carlisle to form one branch of the National Union of Railwaymen. Here officials pose with their new banner. These men took a leading part in the 1926 strike. Seated on the left is Joe Henderson, Carlisle's first Labour Mayor in 1927, later an MP and created a Lord in 1950.

Nothing had stopped the movement of traffic in Carlisle Station until the first national strike in 1911. From then on these became more frequent and disruptive.

For nine days in 1926, it was only volunteers who managed to move essential supplies during the national strike.

Wage disputes between British Railways and rail unions led to strikes by ASLEF and NUR members. Often the unions did not act together and limited services operated.

One day strikes by most railway workers became common in the 1990s prior to privatisation.

Cumberland Evening News 30 May 1955

Bucket and spade at the ready, a boy waits to see if a train would go to Silloth during a 17-day strike in 1955 by ASLEF members.

Right: NUR members organised an effective 24-hour strike in 1962. Shorter strikes became the pattern for the future.

CUMBERLAND EVENING NEWS

CARLISLE, WEDNESDAY, OCTOBER 3, 1962

THE DESERTED STATION as strike stops all trains

"IT'S SOLID!" SAY N.U.R

Carlisle pickets go back home on 'complete success'

HOLIDAYS & SPECIALS

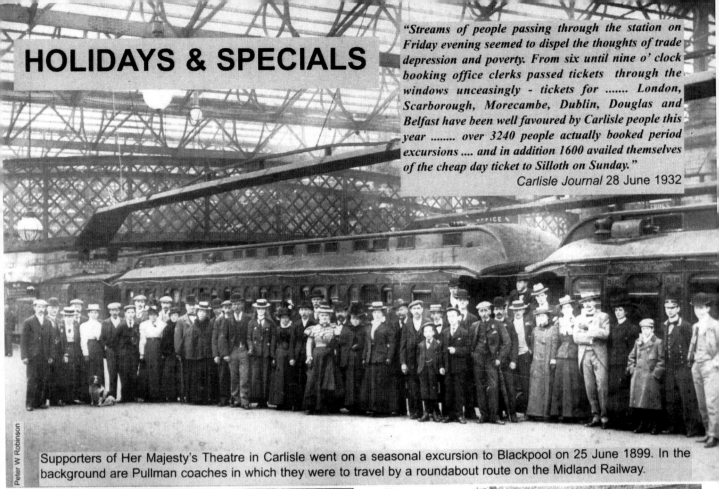

Peter W Robinson

"Streams of people passing through the station on Friday evening seemed to dispel the thoughts of trade depression and poverty. From six until nine o' clock booking office clerks passed tickets through the windows unceasingly - tickets for .... London, Scarborough, Morecambe, Dublin, Douglas and Belfast have been well favoured by Carlisle people this year .... over 3240 people actually booked period excursions .... and in addition 1600 availed themselves of the cheap day ticket to Silloth on Sunday."

Carlisle Journal 28 June 1932

Supporters of Her Majesty's Theatre in Carlisle went on a seasonal excursion to Blackpool on 25 June 1899. In the background are Pullman coaches in which they were to travel by a roundabout route on the Midland Railway.

Carlisle Journal 3 July 1934

One of the busiest times of the year was during Race week in Carlisle. Here on Saturday 30 June 1934 crowds await the departure of the 1.28 pm train to Blackpool.

Carlisle Journal 1 June 1928

Sister Lillie organised trips for deprived children to Silloth. Here in May 1928 a group awaits departure.

There were many unscheduled excursion trains which passed through Carlisle Station at holiday times. Passenger numbers dramatically increased at these busy periods and often broke records.

On 4 August 1911, 4297 people travelled to Silloth. This broke the previous record, which was set on Whit Monday 1906, when 3944 went to Silloth

Carlisle Journal 23 June 1932

Left: Mayor of Carlisle, Matthew Thompson, organised a fund that would allow children of the unemployed a holiday. In June 1932, he says goodbye to those off for a week's holiday at the seaside.

Right: Station Master, James Leslie poses with those about to board a Carr's Biscuit Works special to a pantomime in Newcastle on 31 January 1959.

Alistair Leslie/Cumberland News

EXPRESSES

"The final 300 miles non-stop run this season of the Royal Scot from Euston to Carlisle was signalised on Saturday by a fine achievement. The express lost time slightly on the way from London and passed Lancaster three minutes late, but by the time Tebay was reached one minute had been taken off the arrears and the train ran through Carlisle Station two minutes ahead of time."

Carlisle Journal 24 September 1929

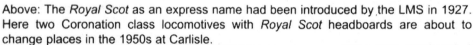

Above: The *Royal Scot* as an express name had been introduced by the LMS in 1927. Here two Coronation class locomotives with *Royal Scot* headboards are about to change places in the 1950s at Carlisle.

Hornby Hobbies

Above right: Headboards from some of the named expresses running on British Railways into Carlisle during the 1950s and early 60s

National Railway Museum / Science & Society Picture Library

Newton Replicas

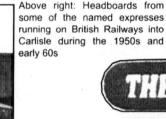

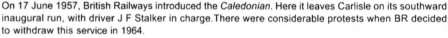

Cumberland News 21 June 1957

On 17 June 1957, British Railways introduced the *Caledonian*. Here it leaves Carlisle on its southward inaugural run, with driver J F Stalker in charge. There were considerable protests when BR decided to withdraw this service in 1964.

There were no named express trains running before grouping in 1923. Passengers in these pre-announcement days must have been adept at getting onto the right train.

To improve their image, certain expresses were given names by the LMS in the 1920s and the *Royal Scot* was an example. Competition with LNER streamlined trains on the East Coast Main Line led to the introduction by the LMS of the streamlined *Coronation Scot*.

With Nationalisation, British Railways revived old express names and new ones which had prominently displayed headboards on the front of locomotives and on the side of each carriage.

There are named expresses running through Carlisle today, but apart from paper carriage labels and mention of the name in announcements, they are not given the same prominence.

Right: The Coronation Scot leaves Carlisle on a southbound journey in 1937.

National Railway Museum / Science & Society Picture Library

Above: The introduction of the *Silver Jubilee* express by the LNER in 1935, showed that streamlined locomotives and carriages could travel at greater speeds between London and Edinburgh. This led to the LMS competing with the *Coronation Scot* which was similarly streamlined.

Tullie House Museum

NAMED LOCOMOTIVES

Left: The Dean of Carlisle, the Right Reverend Henry Stapleton names *Carlisle Cathedral* on 20 September 1997

Mrs G M Griffiths

Class 86 Locomotive Nº 86204 Named CITY OF CARLISLE *at Carlisle Station on Thursday 7ᵗʰ December 1978 by Councillor G. H. GRIFFITHS Mayor of Carlisle*

Divisional Manager Preston British Rail London Midland

British Railways Board / Railtrack PLC

At one time locomotives were given names without any formal ceremony. This changed with Grouping in 1923. However, only one steam engine was named at Carlisle. In the 1930s, when war was imminent, the name of the local regiment was applied with patriotic zeal. It was also intended to name *City of Carlisle* in the station in 1939, but the war intervened.

Only one diesel-electric locomotive was named in the station in 1963, with the new name of the local regiment. An electric locomotive was named *City of Carlisle* by the Mayor in 1978.

A Driving Van Trailer (DVT) was named *Spirit of Cumbria* in the station in 1996 by InterCity West Coast in celebration of the UK Year of Visual Arts. To celebrate 150 years of the Citadel Station an electric locomotive was named *Carlisle Cathedral*, for Virgin Rail, on the station in 1997.

Harry Griffiths, Mayor of Carlisle, names electric locomotive 86204 *City of Carlisle* on 7 December 1978. The plaque shown above right was presented to Councillor Griffiths after the ceremony.

Below left: Nameplates of locomotives named on the station.

Bottom left: The band of the Border Regiment parade beside LMS Royal Scot class 6136, when this was renamed *The Border Regiment* on 6 June 1936.

Right: Correspondence about the naming of Coronation class 6238 *City of Carlisle*.

Below: Colonel Darlington names diesel-electric locomotive D58 *The Kings Own Royal Border Regiment* on 1 May 1963.

THE KINGS OWN ROYAL BORDER REGIMENT

CEN 1 May 1963

Tullie House Museum

Spirit of Cumbria

THE BORDER REGIMENT

King's Own Royal Border Regiment Museum

A RAILWAY ENGINE CHRISTENED

Carlisle Journal 9 June 1936

LONDON MIDLAND AND SCOTTISH RAILWAY COMPANY

COMMERCIAL MANAGER'S OFFICE, CENTRAL STATION (OF UNION STREET),

GLASGOW, C.I.

12th September, 39

Fredk. G. Webster Esq.,
Town Clerk,
Carlisle.

Dear Mr Webster,

NAMING OF ENGINE.

I duly received your letter of 2nd September, and of course in view of war all further steps in the presentation of the engine...

City of Carlisle

8th September, 1939.

TC/HH.

Dear Mr. Yeoman,

New Express Passenger Locomotives.

I take it that in view of the outbreak of war, the proposed naming ceremony for the engines will be cancelled. Both you and I will have far too much important business demanding attention, and I think this ceremony should be postponed or cancelled.

Kindly let me know that you agree.

Yours faithfully,

(SGD.):- FREDK. G. WEBSTER
Town Clerk.

STATION AT WAR

VAD and Red Cross volunteers on parade at the station during World War I.

Each train carried 25 officers, 440 men, six nurses and ten tons of baggage......It was our proud boast that we provided every man with coffee and refreshments at Carlisle Station.

Above: Nicol Campbell was awarded the MBE in 1919 for hi wartime work as Station Superintendent

Below right: World War II poster discouraging civilian rail travel.

IS YOUR JOURNEY REALLY NECESSARY?

TICKETS

National Railway Museum
Science & Society Picture Library

This bomb-proof emergency generator house was built at the station during World War II and is still there today.

During both wars traffic was heavy through the station. Large numbers of troops passed through on their way to the Front and others returned on leave. Refreshments were provided for all who needed them. Wounded soldiers were also refreshed when ambulance trains arrived in the station.

Strict air raid precautions were taken during World War II; the roof glazing was painted black, lighting reduced and air-raid shelters provided in the arches beneath the station. The public were discouraged from travelling and 'holidays at home' were encouraged.

Patt Honeyman

34

Troops awaiting embarkation in 1914 on, what is today, platform 6. Wartime restrictions meant that photographs of troop movements at the station could no longer be taken during World War II

NATIONALISATION

The background map shows the British Railways system

CARLISLE

British Railways 'totem' sign for Carlisle Station

BRITISH RAILWAYS

SCALE OF MILES

Locomotive 'Exchanges' in the 1920s and again in 1948 led to a 'standard' design for British Railways steam locomotives. In 1926, Great Western Railway 5000 *Launceston Castle* leaves Carlisle for trials on the LMS

CARLISLE
Travel there in rail comfort

British Railways poster advertising Carlisle

Under grouping in 1923 the seven companies coming into Carlisle were reduced to just two - the London and North Eastern Railway and the London, Midland and Scottish.

Heavy traffic during the war and lack of replacement of rolling stock left the railway system in need of drastic modernisation.

The incoming Labour Government of 1945 decided to nationalise the 'Big Four' to form British Railways on 1 January 1948. Post-war shortages meant that changes were not immediately made, except in liveries and uniforms.

Under the new British Transport Commission, the Railway Executive divided the country into six regional boards, Carlisle coming within the London Midland Region, but bordered on the Scottish and North Eastern Regions.

It was not until 23 February 1948 that the new livery was first seen in Carlisle.

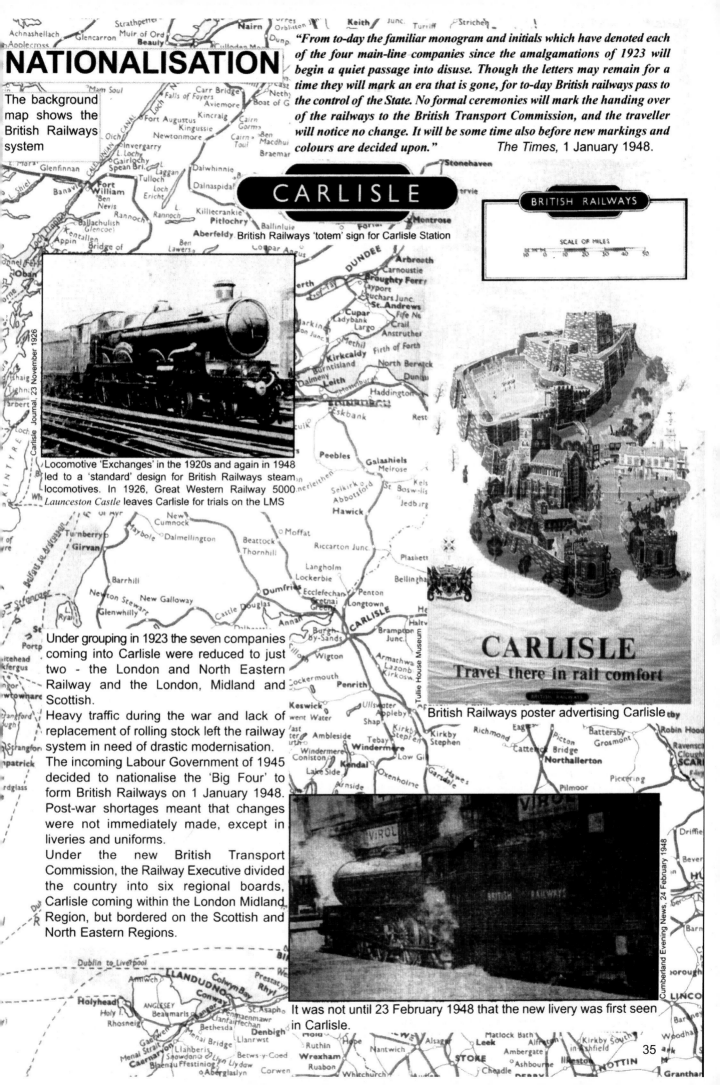

35

TICKET BARRIERS

Right: Tickets collected at the station barrier.

All tickets please!

Tickets had to be collected from passengers outside the station. This meant stopping each train before it entered the station and ticket examiners working their way along the outside of the train.

The station was at first 'open,' which meant that tickets had to be collected before trains arrived. Special ticket platforms were at the north and south of the station, so that ticket examiners could gain access to each carriage compartment. This was not a problem on corridor stock.

Experiments were carried out in World War I and in 1936 to 'close' the station. At night the station had been 'closed' and entry was by ticket only.

Barriers were permanently erected in 1938. Tickets were then collected at these barriers and access to the station was restricted to passengers or platform ticket holders.

Then, in 1984, Carlisle once again became an open station. All tickets are now checked and punched on the trains. The barriers have been removed.

" O.K. then. . . punch their tickets—but remember THAT'S ALL! "

A *Cumberland News* cartoon shows a ticket collector at the barrier and inset is ticket collector Robert Sawyers at work in 1962.

The LNWR ticket platform was just to the south of the station

The ticket platforms merely consisted of a raised wooden walkway

DIESEL DAWN

"British Railways had been subjected to some criticism because they were not moving with the times and that if their services were modernised their progress would be better."
Carlisle Journal 26 November 1954

Officials pose beside the new Diesel Multiple Units (DMUs) on 24 November 1954, for the trial run to Silloth.

John Huggon / CJ 26 November 1954

In 1955 DMUs were introduced on services to Keswick and West Cumberland. DMUs continued on the Silloth line until closure in 1964.

Below left: Driver Herbert Boak expresses his opinion on the DMU service to Silloth.

Carlisle Journal 19 November 1954

This is much better than steam!

Carlisle Journal 26 November 1954

Below: Diesel locomotives 10000 and 10001, still in LMS livery, leave Carlisle pulling the *Royal Scot* for the first time in October 1948.

Two experimental diesel locomotives were introduced for main-line duties by the LMS in 1947. These were first used through Carlisle in 1948.

It was not until 1954 that DMUs were introduced on local stopping services. These proved such a success that their use spread to other lines, being used on the Newcastle route regularly from 1960.

In 1959 the first allocation of main-line diesels was made to Upperby Engine shed and these rapidly took over express workings. The withdrawal of steam locomotives, up to their last use locally on 30 December 1967, saw the exclusive use of diesels from then on.

Since electrification in 1974 it is now rare to see a diesel locomotive pulling a passenger train. High Speed Trains (HSTs) on cross-country services are diesel hauled but the locomotive units form an integral part of the train and are rarely detached.

NEW STRIDE IN TRAIN TRAVEL
Experimental run by Diesels to Carlisle
SPEED, COMFORT, CLEANLINESS

Carlisle Journal, 8 October, 1948

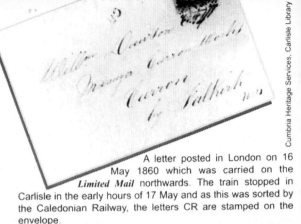

A letter posted in London on 16 May 1860 which was carried on the *Limited Mail* northwards. The train stopped in Carlisle in the early hours of 17 May and as this was sorted by the Caledonian Railway, the letters CR are stamped on the envelope.

Above: Poster for the LMS Night Mail, immortalised in the poem by W H Auden to accompany the 1936 GPO film 'Night Mail': *"This is the Night Mail, crossing the border, bringing the cheque and the postal order."*

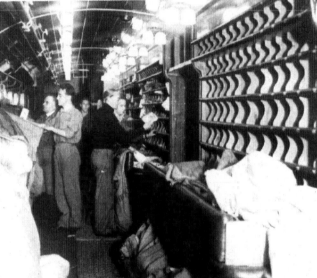

Inside a LMS TPO on a run through Carlisle. Pigeon holes along the sides of the carriage aid sorting.

A TPO in distinctive livery being loaded for a southbound journey at Carlisle Station, 3 June 1996

Victorian postmarks used on TPOs from Carlisle.

Royal Mail had previously been carried by stage coaches, but when the Caledonian Railway opened the main line through Glasgow and beyond, a sorting carriage was attached on a northbound train for the first time on 10 March 1848. Sorting mail on the train speeded delivery.

Today sorting is done on Travelling Post Offices (TPOs) and two such trains leave Carlisle Station each weekday evening to carry letter post south. A similar northbound service, carrying mail from the south, arrives in the early hours of the morning. Hence *"The Night Mail."*

To enable next day delivery of first class post, new Distribution Centres have been opened and a daytime containerised mail train, serving these depots, passes through Carlisle each weekday afternoon.

A new EMU Royal Mail Railnet train picking up containerised post in Carlisle Station on 15 January 1998.

LIVESTOCK & WILDLIFE

Below: Often a special train would bring an entire circus to Carlisle, big top, elephants and all. Here circus horses are coming out of the station into Court Square in the 1950s.

"Rail chiefs desperate to get rid of starlings roosting in Carlisle station have hired pest controllers from Kent to scare them off - with exploding balloons. Dozens of birds are making their homes on girders under the station roof and are creating a nuisance for passengers and station staff."
Cumberland News 9 December 1994

As common carriers up to 1962, railways had to take everything that was offered for transit. This included live animals.

Most animals would travel in goods trains and would not pass through the station. Perishable livestock was taken by passenger train, in the guard's van, or a specially designated carriage attached to a scheduled service.

Today there is no such traffic on the railways, but there is plenty of wildlife in the station. Pigeons have always been there and are no longer regarded as a pest.

Swarms of starlings roosting in the station roof overnight have caused problems in recent years. Various methods have been adopted to scare them away with limited success.

More drastic methods have been used to deal with starlings. This 5 year old Harris Hawk called 'Rolph' and handler have been called in. On one occasion a train was delayed by 16 minutes whilst the hawk was coaxed off the roof of a carriage, where it had settled to devour a starling.

OFF TO HUNT IN THE ISLE OF ARRAN

Otter hounds off to Arran in 1938 and below racing pigeons in 1963.

A decoy owl sits in the station roof over the footbridge to scare starlings. Few passengers notice his presence.

Above: Ready for a 300-mile journey to the point of release, the homing pigeons are carefully placed in baskets to go by rail.

39

MAINTENANCE

Cumbria Heritage Services, Carlisle Library

When this photograph was taken for the 1953 Coronation, the sandstone facade fo the station was blackened by years of smoke pollution.

The Citadel Station in its final rebuilding covered an area of seven acres and was built of stone, metal, timber and glass. These materials needed regular maintenance and the glass occasionally cleaned.

Trackwork needed occasional replacement, mechanical parts

in signals and clocks required cleaning and electrical equipment and plumbing needed regular attention. Station staff were, at first, employed to do this. Later the LNWR and CR took 5-year turns at maintenance until 1923. Years of corrosive smoke had its effects on the stonework, requiring both cleaning and replacement. The final withdrawal of steam afforded the opportunity to use a more imaginative colour scheme on the remaining roof metalwork.

Cumberland News 6 June 1958

Above: For the Octocentenary celebration in June 1958, Frank Sewell paints the coat of arms over the station entrance, the first time they had ever been coloured.

Cumberland News 25 November 1955

High above the Court Square, a workman prepares the Station clock tower for repairs and cleaning.

Carlisle Journal 24 March 1936

Much of the summer of 1936 was spent in painting the woodwork of the end screens and station roof. This was to be the last time that it was to be done.

Citadel Station Joint Committee minutes show that, on 27 June 1890, painting was authorised at a cost of £2083 3s 8d. Minutes noted that this was last done in 1885 for £1931 12s 3d. Maintenance was not so regular in the 20th century.

Cumberland News 17 January 1964

Above: Regular painting of the roof metalwork was necessary. Here, in 1964, A. Eaves and F. McManus work from plank decking high in the roof.

Left: Cleaning the central facade of the station in 1955 and 1956 revealed weathered stone which needed replacement. In November 1955, a mason works from scaffolding around the clock tower.

This aerial view, taken on 22 September 1955, shows Carlisle Citadel Station in its setting. The Victoria Viaduct crosses the north end of the station, with Little and Ballantyne's seed merchants on the left. One of the circular towers of the Courts (the former Citadel) overlooks Court Square. The central painted building is the County Hotel. Work on replacing the glazing of the station roof is in progress. Small black squares are where panes of glass are missing. The north screen is blackened by smoke. Photograph by permission of Aerofilms Ltd..

REMOVING THE ROOF

START OF £200,000 JOB

Carlisle Journal 17 September 1954

Press coverage of the replacement of the roof in 1954. This was the first phase of a much larger scheme.

AFTER

Ashley Kendall

Platform 1 was originally covered by the overall roof of 1880. This can be seen in the photograph of 1936, left. A more recent photograph, above, from the same location, shows open sky where the roof was removed in 1957 and replaced by a low level platform canopy.

BEFORE

Tullie House Museum

Work in progress, removing the roof from platform 1 in 1957. Piles of timber from the roof await disposal.

Such a large glass roof had always presented problems to the Joint Station Committee. Minutes show that 90 square feet of glass was blown out in gales on 27 December 1898. This necessitated replacement of all the glass in 1901 at a cost of £21, 637.

During World War II the station was badly neglected, particularly the roof. The timber was not painted and, in the early 1950s, it began to rot. Fear of falling glass was a constant threat.

Work began in 1954 to replace a central section of the roof with modern steel framed glazing and this was completed in 1955. Then in 1957 the remaining overall roof was removed from platform 1 and the rest cut back at either end. The newly exposed platforms were then covered by low level canopies and new end screens were added.

British Railways Board/Railtrack PLC

BEFORE

Above is a composite photograph taken in the early 1950s of the smoke-blackened north screen of 1880. Right is a 1996 view from the same location showing what was removed in 1957.

42   **AFTER**

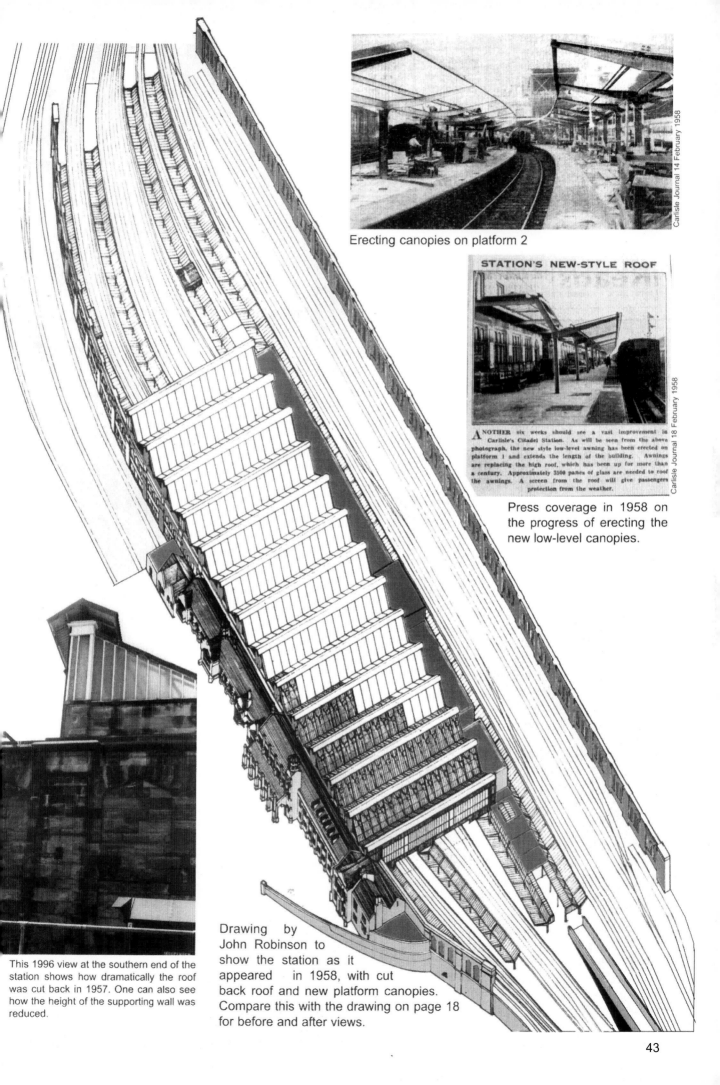

Carlisle Journal 14 February 1958

Erecting canopies on platform 2

Carlisle Journal 18 February 1958

STATION'S NEW-STYLE ROOF

ANOTHER six weeks should see a vast improvement in Carlisle's Citadel Station. As will be seen from the above photograph, the new style low-level awning has been erected on platform 1 and extends the length of the building. Awnings are replacing the high roof, which has been up for more than a century. Approximately 3500 panes of glass are needed to roof the awnings. A screen from the roof will give passengers protection from the weather.

Press coverage in 1958 on the progress of erecting the new low-level canopies.

This 1996 view at the southern end of the station shows how dramatically the roof was cut back in 1957. One can also see how the height of the supporting wall was reduced.

Drawing by John Robinson to show the station as it appeared in 1958, with cut back roof and new platform canopies. Compare this with the drawing on page 18 for before and after views.

1958 EXHIBITION

Built in 1892 LNWR 790 *Hardwicke*, was of an earlier design. This did not prevent it from taking part in the railway races from London to Aberdeen in 1895, when it covered the section from Crewe to Carlisle at an average speed of 67.2 mph. Beyond is CR123 and the tender of LNWR 3020 *Cornwall* is on the left.

A replica of Stephenson's Rocket was on display.

Cumberland News 6 June & 25 April 1958

"Dandy" coming back to Carlisle

LETTERS TO THE EDITOR

On 7 June 1958 a temporary exhibition of historic railway vehicles opened in the station. This was the highlight of celebrations to mark Carlisle's Octocentenary as a city and would be seen by the Queen when she entered the city by rail in July; to take part in the celebrations. As it was she was ill and did not come until the exhibition was over.

The exhibits, many from York Railway Museum, were arranged on the rails of platform 6 and along the platform surface. There were carriages, locomotives, models, replicas and numerous smaller exhibits. Never before, or since, has there been such an exhibition in the city.

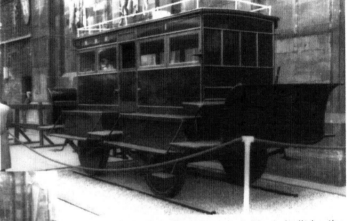

Above: Port Carlisle Dandy coach No.1, built by the NBR in 1856 and used on the Port Carlisle branch between 1859 and 1914. When the exhibition ended this was moved to the end of platforms 5 & 6 as a permanent exhibit, until recalled in 1969. It returned briefly for exhibition in the station in 1986.

Above: Furness Railway No.3 *Coppernob* was exhibited on a well waggon.

Right: Two royal train carriages, built for Queen Victoria by the LNWR in 1869, were rebuilt as one vehicle in 1895. This would have been regularly used for the Queen's journeys through Carlisle. Other royal carriages were also exhibited.

44

ENTHUSIASTS AND PRESERVED STEAM

Cumberland Evening News 4 April 1963

Train spotters hail city stationmaster

I DON'T know whether or not you heard a broadcast programme the other day, but featured in it was Mr J. S. Leslie, Carlisle's stationmaster. He was asked his opinion about train-spotters, and his replies, I hear, have earned him recognition from a Midlands train spotting club!

It seems that Mr Leslie's sensible views on the subject so impressed the club that the members felt they must do him honour.

So they have sent him a letter expressing their appreciation of his views.

Places of interest

What did Mr Leslie say on the air? Merely that he welcomed the interest of any genuine train spotter and, provided they behave themselves, he would not move towards barring them from his station. Did they misbehave then they

WHAT MR LESLIE SAID

Providing boys behave themselves I do not mind them trainspotting in the station.

Above, a typical friendly spotter

Station Master James Leslie welcomed train spotters to the city at a time in the early 1960s when vandalism had got them a bad name and they had been banned from other main-line stations.

Crowds admire 60532 *Blue Peter*, which hauled a charter train over the Settle and Carlisle line on 14 February 1998.

SCHOOLBOY'S DREAM COMES TRUE

Cumberland News 25 April 1958

Fantastic, this is what I want to do when I grow up !

Colin Armstrong is allowed to take control of a steam locomotive in the station on a visit by Kirkandrews-on-Eden school, 24 April 1958.

Cumberland News 13 June 1958

Children visiting the Octocentenary exhibition in 1958 were allowed onto the exhibits. Here Winifred Carruthers, Veronica Bell and Dora Raffles show that girls were just as interested as boys.

As an important rail centre, Carlisle had always been a Mecca for those interested in railways. The variety of locomotives in the station and the volume of traffic ensured that there was plenty to attract train spotters.

Now many railway enthusiasts and day trippers are brought to the city on steam charter trains.

Left: Black '5' 44767, now named *George Stephenson*, stands at platform 1 after hauling a steam charter from Hull on 14 February 1998. This had been a Carlisle engine from Kingmoor shed. It is now unusual to find two steam locomotives entering the station on the same day. See *Blue Peter* above.

ELECTRIFICATION & TRACTION

DANGER

OVERHEAD LIVE WIRES

Due to the installation of overhead wires in the station, it was necessary to raise the height of the station footbridge.

British Railways Board/Railtrack PLC

Border Press Agency

The Queen and Prince Philip travelled north to Scotland on the day of the switch to electrification. From Lancaster to Oxenholme they were in the cab of the electric locomotive pulling the royal train. After an overnight stop near Carlisle, they arrived in the station on 7 May 1974, for a private 20 minute tour of an exhibition train featuring the newly electrified line. John Wade, Lord Lieutenant, accompanies the Queen to the exhibition.

One of the improvements resulting from electrification of the track was the building of a new signal box at the south end of the station; which came into use in 1973. This box replaced the control room in the station and all of the other signal boxes in the area.

The second part of Dr. Beeching's report, published in February 1965, envisaged that by 1984 the West Coast line would be the only direct route to Scotland. It was thus essential for this line to be electrified over its whole length. The section from London to Crewe was completed in 1966 and the Government sanctioned electrification northwards to Glasgow in 1970.

Power on the newly electrified section was switched on for the opening on 6 May 1974. Not all the lines running into Carlisle are electrified and diesel locomotives are frequent visitors, particularly on freight workings.

A crash on the Avoiding Goods Lines on 1 May 1984 led to their immediate closure. All freight traffic now passes through the station; which has resulted in minor re-arrangement of trackwork.

Left: As there are now no engine sheds in the city, diesel engines have been stabled in the former carriage sidings alongside platform 1. It has thus been necessary to provide accommodation for train crews within former offices on platform 1.

Ian Parsons

REGIONAL RAILWAYS

TRAIN CREW ACCOMMODATION

Right: The *Cumberland News* in 1971 foresaw the competition between the newly completed M6 motorway and an electrified main line

CN 3 December 1971

Electrification - opening up Cumbria to the nation

By DAVID CUITE

Completion of the M6 motorway marked the beginning of the end for the years of semi-isolationism in which Cumbria as a region had been wrapped. And now the electrification of the main railway line promises to open it up completely, bringing the rest of the nation closer.

...leaping ahead by up to 60 per cent. Now, with the experience of this successful first stage behind them, British Rail's engineers are electrifying the rest of the route from Crewe to Glasgow, and this of course, means a great deal of work in Cumbria... completed

...isation. Much of the work is carried out on Sundays, thereby minimising diversions and delays.

One of the biggest problems both at the planning and construction stages, has been that of dealing with the many bridges that span the line. To provide the necessary headroom for the overhead cables...

...the continuous and hea... fic. Cost of this work w... million and it involve... 45,056 tons of new ... 540,000 concrete sle...

The existing, s... primitive signalling... ments being conve... incredibly complex... ishingly reliable... system.

Gone will be all... track side s...

DR BEECHING AND THE END OF STEAM

British Railways Board/Railtrack PLC

BRITISH RAILWAYS BOARD

The Reshaping of British Railways

PART 1: REPORT

There's no need for a railway to Silloth.

Rail axe shatters docks expansion hopes

BEECHING 'BLOW' TO TOURISM
Fears rise in Silloth and Lakes

MANY people in the Border area, particularly those in the tourist industry, are worried by Dr Richard Beeching's plan to reshape British Railways.

BEECHING PLAN
PROPOSALS FOR LINES IN NORTHWEST AREA—PASSENGER SERVICES

Cumberland News 22, 29 March 1963

LIST FOR THE AXE

This is the end of the line for me.

Local press opinion on the Beeching report

Dr Beeching and his 1963 report.

Dr Richard Beeching was appointed in May 1961, as Chairman of the British Transport Commission (British Railways Board from the 1 January 1963), by a Government increasingly concerned at the rising annual deficit of the railways. British Railways had paid their way until 1957, but then operated at a loss. This could not continue.

The Beeching Report, published on 27 March 1963, showed that over half the total income accounted for only 4% of passenger miles. It was recommended that inter-city services be improved and that 5,000 miles of revenue losing lines should be closed, along with 2,000 stations. Not all of the report was implemented, but where it was, the pace was considered indecent.

In 1955, a modernisation plan was published in which the key features were the abolition of steam locomotives in favour of diesel and electric traction. This was to be phased over a period of 15 years.

All this led to a drastic reduction in the number of staff and Carlisle's importance as a railway centre diminished.

Above: Rail services to Edinburgh were replaced by a courtesy bus in 1969, when the Waverley line closed. This had been recommended by Dr Beeching

Bottom left and right: Steam locomotives ceased to be used on trains in Carlisle on 30 December 1967. However, as a final gesture to the national withdrawal of steam, a special train was run to Carlisle on 11 August 1968, pulled in by 70013 *Oliver Cromwell*.
The train then returned southwards hauled by two Black '5's. Crowds gathered on the station platforms to witness the event.

City's farewell to steam era

Cumberland News 16 August 1968

A change of engines and the last steam train to run in Great Britain for British Rail pulls out of Carlisle station. It was watched by hundreds of spectators. More pictures on Page 6.

47

THEN AND NOW

Tullie House Museum

A view of the north-west corner of the station, taken from the Viaduct in 1930. Below, the same view in 1996 shows how roof removal has reduced the height of the west side of the station.

An Edinburgh train awaits departure in the early 1920s, hauled by NBR 904. The photograph below shows the same viewpoint on platform 8 in 1996.

Right: Midland Railway locomotives double-head a southbound express, taken about 1902.

Above right: The same view taken in 1996 on platform 3 when two electric locomotives were in a similar location.

Two LNWR locomotives have been attached to this southbound train, which would have come from Glasgow. The date is about 1902.

Below: The same location on platform 4 in 1996.

Caledonian Railway, *Cardean* class 904, built in 1906, seen at the north end of the station, adjacent to platform 1. At the right is Hudson Scott's metal box factory, which dates the photograph to before 1911. Below: The view from the same point in 1996.

Maryport & Carlisle Railway No.13 stands at the south end of the station on 29 April 1910, one of a series of photographs taken to mark the retirement of William Haythornthwaite as Station Superintendent; he is seen in top hat on the left. The inset shows the same location in 1996; now platform 2.

49

IMPROVEMENTS AND THE FUTURE

Below: Improvements made by InterCity West Coast were a new ticket office and concourse opened in 1989. This was made possible by the removal of ticket barriers in 1984.

This facility is operated by InterCity West Coast Limited

From 1982 the station was operated by InterCity West Coast Limited, a subsidiary of British Rail.

This plaque was unveiled by Her Royal Highness the Duchess of York on Friday 7th April 1989 to commemorate the opening of the new Ticket Hall

Media interest in the arrival of the first Virgin CrossCountry service in Carlisle from Edinburgh on 6 January 1997 and an end to nationalisation.

There were fears in the early 1980s with the introduction of the Advanced Passenger Train (APT), which was not to stop in the city, that Carlisle's importance as a railway centre would diminish. Technical problems and union pressure led to the abandonment of the APT.

On 4 January 1982, British Rail was split into five independent sectors, Carlisle coming within the operating area of InterCity West Coast Limited. They initiated changes to the station to improve its image and make it more user friendly.

During the mid-1990s run up to de-nationalisation, locomotive liveries changed, bringing back to the station a diversity of colour which had not been seen since 1923. Freight services are now operated by different franchise holders and their individual liveries have maintained this diversity. With de-nationalisation Virgin Rail acquired the franchise for Cross Country and InterCity West Coast in 1997. It is proposed by Virgin to introduce High Speed Trains (HSTs), which will tilt on curves and allow faster speeds, similar to the APT.

CN 5 December 1997

Virgin plan more tilt trains on county lines

RAIL bosses are to consider introducing ... field ...
sider ... of
mph ...

Carlisle Post 8 August 1985

STATION'S FUTURE IS SECURED

Carlisle axe threat denied by manager

The future of main-
Car... tion
lin...

... number of improvements to
the service ... also quick
Mr Ha... out that from
... September there is
... morning train
... Preston ...

rives in Carlisle at 8.15 a.m
... feel that this train
will be ideal for students
and shoppers or even ...
... who want to spend a full
day in the City " he said
"I feel that the commuters
have over-reacted and got
hold of completely
... the proposals were put
... to the country council be
cause we have an accepted
procedure for consultation
... them but really they
... them but ... adjustments
... just ... adjustments
... to the existing timetable
... added

NON-STOP TRAIN

BRITISH Rail have announced that the Advanced Passenger Train will begin a regular daily round trip from Glasgow to London in October — but it won't be stopping in Carlisle.

The APT, which will clip 50 minutes off the journey, will come into full service next spring.

However, city MP Ron Lewis, who is sponsored by the National Union of Railwaymen, believes that the APT fleet will eventually stop at Carlisle.

There were fears that Carlisle's importance as a railway centre would be further diminished if the ultra-modern trains failed to stop in the city.

Cumberland Gazette, 2 May 1982

Left: Press reaction to rail plans which would affect Carlisle.

I am confident this country will have in Virgin Rail one of the finest train services the world can offer.

Virgin Rail

Richard Branson, head of Virgin Rail, was confident in 1997 about the future of his rail network. His aim was: "to see the M6 grassed over."

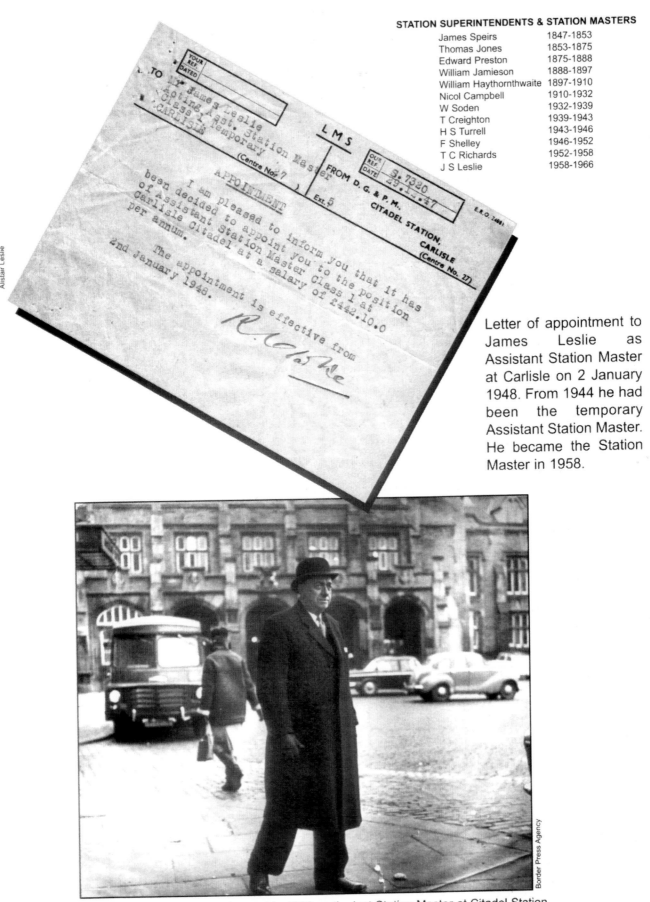

STATION SUPERINTENDENTS & STATION MASTERS

James Speirs	1847-1853
Thomas Jones	1853-1875
Edward Preston	1875-1888
William Jamieson	1888-1897
William Haythornthwaite	1897-1910
Nicol Campbell	1910-1932
W Soden	1932-1939
T Creighton	1939-1943
H S Turrell	1943-1946
F Shelley	1946-1952
T C Richards	1952-1958
J S Leslie	1958-1966

Letter of appointment to James Leslie as Assistant Station Master at Carlisle on 2 January 1948. From 1944 he had been the temporary Assistant Station Master. He became the Station Master in 1958.

James Leslie walks away to retirement in 1966 as the last Station Master at Citadel Station

OTHER LOCAL BOOKS AVAILABLE FROM P3 PUBLICATIONS

Title	ISBN	First published
Carlisle's First Learning Centre: Tullie House	978-09934889-0-0	2016
The Carlisle Floods 2015 with recollections of 2005	978-09934889-1-7	2016
Cumbrian Ancestors Unwrapped	978-09572412-6-8	2014
Allonby A short history and Guide	978-09572412-7-5	2014
The Carlisle Ship Canal 1821 - 1853	978-09572412-4-4	2013
A Century Around Silloth	978-09572412-3-7	2012
Chanel and the Tweedmaker Weavers of Dreams	978-0-9572412-2-0	September 2012
Watching over Carlisle 140 years of the Carlisle City Police Force 1827- 1967	978-0-9559017-6-8	July 2011
Wetheral and Great Corby an illustrated history	978-09559017-2-0	October 2008
More Plain People and places on the Cumbrian Solway Plain	978-09548823-2-7	2007
For more books and further details go to **http://www.p3publications.com** Books can be purchased online using Paypal or credit/debit card through Paypal		